Swisscellany

facts & figures about Switzerland

Diccon Bewes

Swisscellany

facts & figures about Switzerland

Diccon Bewes

© 2012 Bergli Books, Basel
© cover and illustrations Mischa Kammermann, Basel

Bergli Books   Tel.: +41 61 373 27 77
CH-4001 Basel   e-mail: info@bergli.ch
Switzerland   www.bergli.ch

ISBN 978-3-905252-47-7 digital edition
ISBN 978-3-905252-24-8 print edition

For Georgie, Thomas
Rhian and Olivia

Foreword

Look up miscellany in a dictionary and you'll see that it is a group, collection or mixture of different items, ingredients or things. As a noun it's far less used than the adjective derived from it – miscellaneous – which is probably why the British and Americans can't agree on how to pronounce it: I say mis-sel-la-nee, stressing the 'sel'; they say mis-sa-lay-nee, stressing the 'lay'. Collection is probably easier.

This Swiss miscellany is a collection of curious and quirky, statistical and historical, intriguing and interesting facts about Switzerland. It is a subjective look at a unique country and its people, but not an utterly comprehensive one. You can discover how much yoghurt an average Swiss person eats each year but not which flavours, or who was elected president the most times but not who voted for him, and even the most successful pop songs but not why anyone bought them.

So just dive in and maybe discover a few things about Switzerland you never knew. At the very least, you'll be able to sing along to the Swiss national anthem, even if no-one else does.

Swisscellany

Switzerland in Brief

Area	41,285km²	(134th in the world, similar to The Netherlands)
Population	7,870,100	(95th in the world, similar to Israel)
Boundary	1,899km	
Border with		
Italy	744km	
France	572km	
Germany	362km	
Austria	180km	
Liechtenstein	41km	

Place furthest from the national border	Uttigen (BE), 69km
Highest point	Dufourspitze* 4634m
Lowest point	Ascona 193m
Average height	1307m
Distance north to south	224km
Northernmost point (SH)	47° 48′ 30″ N, 8° 34′ 5″ E
Southernmost point (TI)	45° 49′ 4″ N, 9° 1′ 0.8″ E
Midpoint of Switzerland	Älggialp (OW) 46° 48′ 4″ N, 8° 13′ 36″ E
Distance west to east	352km
Westernmost point (GE)	46° 7′ 56″ N, 5° 57′ 21″ E
Easternmost point (GR)	46° 36′ 55″ N, 10° 29′ 32″ E

*Also known as Monte Rosa

Did you know?
If Switzerland were ironed out so that it was all at the same elevation, its surface area would increase by 5,200km² or 12.5% – equivalent to adding another canton the size of Valais.

Swiss on Board the Titanic

The Titanic sank on 15 April 1912 with the loss of 1,514 lives. Of the 25 Swiss passengers and crew on board, 12 survived.

Died on the Titanic	Class	Age
[1]Charles Williams-White	1st	51
Josef Arnold-Franchi	3rd	25
Josefine Arnold-Franchi	3rd	18
Aloisia Haas	3rd	24
Albert Wirz	3rd	27
Narciso Bazzi	Crew	33
Joseph Bochatay	Crew	30
Gérald Grosclaude	Crew	24
Adolf Mattmann	Crew	20
Alessandro Pedrini	Crew	21
Abele Rigozzi	Crew	22
Johannes Vögelin-Dubach	Crew	35
Mario Zanetti	Crew	20

Did you know?
Born in Geneva, Richard Norris Williams II was an American tennis player who went on to win six Grand Slam titles, including the US Open men's singles in 1914 and 1916, and a gold medal at the 1924 Olympic Games.

Survived on the Titanic	Class	Age	Lived until
Margaret Frölicher-Stehli	1st	48	1955
Maximilian Frölicher-Stehli	1st	60	1913
Margaritha Frölicher	1st	22	1972
Emma Sägesser	1st	24	1964
Alfons Simonius-Blumer	1st	56	1920
Max Staehelin-Maeglin	1st	32	1968
[2]Richard Norris Williams II	1st	21	1968
Marie Jerwan-Thuillard	2nd	23	1974
Bertha Lehmann	2nd	17	1967
[1]Anton Kink-Heilmann	3rd	29	1959
[1]Luise Kink-Heilmann	3rd	26	1979
[2]Luise Kink	3rd	4	1992

[1]Not a Swiss national but long-term resident in Switzerland.
[2]Not a Swiss national but born in Switzerland.

Roger Federer's Grand Slams

Roger Federer has appeared in 23 Grand Slam finals (including a record 10 consecutive ones, 2005 Wimbledon to 2007 US Open). Of the seven he lost, all were to Rafael Nadal except for the 2009 US Open, won by Juan Martin del Potro. He was also ranked as Number One men's player for a record 237 consecutive weeks (February 2004 to August 2008).

Wimbledon

2003	Mark Philippoussis (Aus)	7-6, 6-2, 7-6
2004	Andy Roddick (USA)	4-6, 7-5, 7-6, 6-4
2005	Andy Roddick (USA)	6-2, 7-6, 6-4
2006	Rafael Nadal (Spa)	6-0, 7-6, 6-7, 6-3
2007	Rafael Nadal (Spa)	7-6, 4-6, 7-6, 2-6, 6-2
2009	Andy Roddick (USA)	5-7, 7-6, 7-6, 3-6, 16-14

Australian Open

2004	Marat Safin (Rus)	7-6, 6-4, 6-2
2006	Marcos Baghdatis (Cyp)	5-7, 7-5, 6-0, 6-2
2007	Fernando González (Chi)	7-6, 6-4, 6-4
2010	Andy Murray (UK)	6-3, 6-4, 7-6

US Open

2004	Lleyton Hewitt (Aus)	6-0, 7-6, 6-0
2005	Andre Agassi (USA)	6-3, 2-6, 7-6, 6-1
2006	Andy Roddick (USA)	6-2, 4-6, 7-5, 6-1
2007	Novak Djokovic (Ser)	7-6, 7-6, 6-4
2008	Andy Murray (UK)	6-2, 7-5, 6-2

French Open

| 2009 | Robin Söderling (Swe) | 6-1, 7-6, 6-4 |

Did you know?

The first Swiss player to win any Grand Slam tennis title was Heinz Günthardt, who won the 1981 French Open men's doubles (with Balázs Taróczy of Hungary). He won again with the same partner at Wimbledon in 1985, along with two mixed doubles titles with Martina Navratilova (1985, French Open and US Open).

Did you know?

Martina Hingis was born in Czechoslovakia but moved to Switzerland when she was seven. In 1996 she became the young-est ever winner of any Grand Slam tennis title by winning the women's doubles at Wimbledon aged 15 years and 282 days. She won a total of 15 Grand Slam titles.

Communities by Area

There are 2,495 communities in Switzerland. Canton Bern has the most with 382, whereas Cantons Glarus and Basel-Stadt have only three each. The ten largest communities together make up an area almost the same size as Ticino.

Ten largest communities by area	Canton	km²	Population
Glarus Süd	GL	430.2	9,820
Davos	GR	284.0	11,166
Bagnes	VS	282.3	7,726
Bregaglia	GR	251.5	1,601
Anniviers	VS	243.0	2,617
Zermatt	VS	242.7	5,720
Evolène	VS	209.9	1,683
Zernez	GR	203.9	1,140
Blenio	TI	202.1	1,697
Guttannen	BE	200.8	310
Ten smallest communities by area			
Rivaz	VD	0.31	355
Kaiserstuhl	AG	0.32	398
Gottlieben	TG	0.33	300
Meyriez	FR	0.34	600
Ponte Tresa	TI	0.41	773
Carabietta	TI	0.46	113
Paudex	VD	0.48	1,393
Senèdes	FR	0.50	122
Mauraz	VD	0.50	54
Muralto	TI	0.60	2,769

What the Swiss Eat

The average Swiss person ate a total of 709.8kg of food in 2010, or roughly 13.5kg a week. Dairy products constitute about 20% of the Swiss diet.

kilo per year*		kilo per year*	
Fresh vegetables	78.2	Sugar	40.5
Fresh fruit	**77.6**	Wine	36.5
Apples	17.7	Cheese	21.5
Bananas	9.2	Oil	18.8
Berries	6.8	Yoghurt	18.2
Milk	70.7	Fruit juice	12.8
Wheat	61.0	Eggs	10.8
Beer	56.7	Coffee	9.8
Meat	**53.6**	Fish	8.8
Pork	25.3	Cream	8.1
Beef	11.2	Rice	5.0
Poultry	11.0	Butter	5.4
Potatoes	45.6	Nuts	3.7
Sugar	40.5	Tea	0.3

*liquids are in litres per year

Did you know?

Switzerland has the world's highest annual chocolate consumption – 11.9 kg per head. That's about 33g a day.

The Federal Council

Switzerland's government is a council of Seven Wise Men and (since 1984) Women elected by parliament. 115 Federal Councillors have been elected since the new constitution of 1848.

The original Federal Council*, elected 16 November 1848

†Daniel-Henri Druey	VD	Department of Justice & Police
†Stefano Franscini	TI	Department of Home Affairs
Heidrich Frey-Herosé	AG	Department of Trade & Customs
†Jonas Furrer	ZH	Political Department
†Martin Munzinger	SO	Department of Finance
Wilhelm Matthias Naeff	SG	Department of Posts & Construction
Ulrich Ochsenbein	BE	Department of Defence & Military

*all seven were from the FDP

Shortest terms of office

†Louis Perrier	FDP	NE	1912-1913	1 yr, 2 months, 4 days
Rudolf Friedrich	FDP	ZH	1982-1984	1 yr, 10 months, 12 days
Max Weber	SP	ZH	1951-1953	1 yr, 11 months, 25 days

Longest terms of office

†Karl Schenk	FDP	BE	1863-1895	31 yrs, 7 months, 6 days
†Adolf Deucher	FDP	TG	1883-1912	29 yrs, 3 months
†Giuseppe Motta	CVP	TI	1911-1940	28 yrs, 1 month, 9 days

† Died in office.

First councillor from a party other than the FDP
Joseph Zemp (CVP, LU) elected 1891

First female councillor
Elisabeth Kopp (FDP, ZH) elected 1984

Only native Romansh speaker
Felix Calonder (FDP, GR) elected 1913

Youngest Councillors elected

Numa Droz	FDP	NE	1875	31 yrs, 10 months, 21 days
Jakob Stämpfli	FDP	BE	1854	34 yrs, 9 months, 13 days
Ruth Metzler-Arnold	CVP	AI	1999	34 yrs, 9 months, 16 days

Oldest Councillors elected

Gustave Ador	LP	GE	1917	71 yrs, 6 months, 3 days
Josef Escher	CVP	VS	1950	64 yrs, 11 months, 28 days
Christoph Blocher	SVP	ZH	2003	63 yrs, 1 month, 29 days

Federal Councillors by canton

20	Zurich
14	Bern, Vaud
9	Neuchâtel
7	Ticino
6	Solothurn
5	Aargau, Geneva, Lucerne, St Gallen
4	Fribourg, Graubünden
3	Thurgau, Valais
2	Appenzell Ausserrhoden, Appenzell Innerrhoden, Basel-Stadt, Zug
1	Basel-Land, Glarus, Obwalden

Jura, Nidwalden, Schaffhausen, Schwyz, and Uri
have never had a Federal Councillor elected.

Federal Councillors by party

FDP	69	SVP	9
CVP	20	BDP	2*
SP	14	LP	1

*Samuel Schmid and Eveline Widmer Schlumpf were elected in 2007 as SVP candidates but later joined the BDP.

†Federal Councillors who died in office

		Term of office	Age
Daniel-Henri Druey	VD	1848-55	55
Josef Munzinger	SO	1848-55	63
Stefano Franscini	TI	1848-57	60
Jonas Furrer	ZH	1848-61	56
Karl Schenk	BE	1863-95	71
Victor Ruffy	VD	1867-69	46
Johann Jakob Scherer	ZH	1872-78	53
Fridolin Anderwert	TG	1875-80	52
Wilhelm Hertenstein	ZH	1879-88	63
Louis Ruchonnet	VD	1881-93	59
Adolf Deucher	TG	1883-1912	81
Walter Hauser	ZH	1888-1902	65
Eduard Müller	BE	1895-1919	70
Ernst Brenner	BS	1897-1911	54
Josef Anton Schobinger	LU	1908-11	62
Giuseppe Motta	TI	1911-40	68
Louis Perrier	NE	1912-13	63
Karl Scheurer	BE	1919-29	57
Markus Feldmann	BE	1951-58	61

Fridolin Anderwert (FDP, TG) committed suicide on Christmas Day 1880, soon after being elected President. Press reports about his weight and private life didn't help his state of mind, and he shot himself on the Kleine Schanze in Bern. In his suicide note he wrote "They want a victim, they should have it."

Switzerland at Eurovision

Switzerland has twice hosted the Eurovision Song Contest: the first ever one in 1956 in Lugano and in 1989 in Lausanne.

Winner!

1956	Lys Assia	Refrain
1988	Céline Dion	Ne Partez Pas Sans Moi

2nd place	3 times	12th place	3 times
3rd place	3 times	13th place	3 times
4th place	5 times	14th place	1 time
5th place	2 times	15th place	2 times
6th place	3 times	16th place	3 times
7th place	0 times	17th place	2 times
8th place	5 times	19th place	1 time
9th place	1 time	20th place	1 time
10th place	2 times	22nd place	2 times
11th place	1 time	25th place	2 times

Nul points

1964	Anita Traviersi	I Miei Pensieri
1967	Géraldine	Quel Coeur Vas-tu Briser?
1998	Gunvor	Lass Ihn

Relegated   1995, 1999, 2001, 2003
Semi-final   2004, 2007, 2008, 2009, 2010, 2012
Last place   1964, 1967, 1974, 1998, 2004, 2010, 2011

53 entries

French	24 – including both winners
Italian	11
German	10
English	7
Romansh	1 – Viver Senza Tei sung by Furbaz in 1989. It came 13th out of 22 countries, with 47 points.

Climbing the Mountains

Some notable first ascents of famous Swiss peaks

Jungfrau	3.8.1811	J. & H. Meyer, *J. Bortis, A. Volker*
Wetterhorn	31.8.1844	M. Banholzer, J.Jaun
Piz Bernina	13.9.1850	J. Coaz, J. & L. Tscharner
Dufourspitze	1.8.1855	J. Bibeck, C. Hudson, C. & J. Smith, E. Stevenson, *U. Lauener, J & M. Zumtaugwald*
Mönch	15.8.1857	S. Prages, *C. Almer, U. & C. Kaufmann*
Eiger	11.8.1858	C. Barrington, *C. Almer, P. Bohren*
Aletschhorn	18.6.1859	F. Tuckett, *J. Bennen, P. Bohren, V. Tairraz*
Weisshorn	19.8.1861	J. Tindall, *J. Benet, U. Wenger*
Dent Blanche	18.7.1862	T. Kennedy, W. Wigram, *J. Croz, J. Kronig*
Matterhorn	14.7.1865	Lord F. Douglas, D. Hadow, C. Hudson, E. Whymper, *M. Croz, P & P Taugwalder*
Eiger North Face	21.7.1938	H. Harrer, A. Heckmair, F. Kasparek, L. Vörg

Swiss guides in Italics

Did you know?

In 1855 British mountaineer Reverend Charles Hudson was one of the team that conquered Switzerland's highest peak and was also the first to climb Mont Blanc (in France) without any guides. Ten years later he fell to his death – along with Croz, Douglas and Hadow – after successfully climbing the Matterhorn.

The Geneva Conventions

194 countries have signed the Geneva Conventions, the most recent being Montenegro in 2006.

First: Convention for the Amelioration of the Condition of the Sick and Wounded in Armed Forces in the Field.
Original adoption 1864.
64 articles & 2 annexes

Second: Convention for the Amelioration of the Condition of Wounded, Sick and Shipwrecked Members of Armed Forces at Sea.
Original adoption 1907.
63 articles & 1 annexe

Third: Convention relative to the Treatment of Prisoners of War.
Original adoption 1929.
143 articles & 5 annexes

Fourth: Convention relative to the Protection of Civilian Persons in Time of War.
Original adoption 1949.
159 articles & 3 annexes

Did you know?
The first Geneva Convention of 1864 was replaced by later versions, most recently in 1949, but it remained in force until 1966. That was when all the countries to have signed it had also acceded to the newest version. The last country to do so was the Republic of Korea.

Switzerland at the Olympics

Switzerland has twice hosted the Winter Games, both times in St Moritz, in 1928 & 1948 and is home to the International Olympic Committee (in Lausanne).

Overall the Swiss have won a total of 305 medals at the Summer & Winter Olympic Games, making them 16th in the unofficial overall medals' table.

Medals table

	Gold	Silver	Bronze	Total
Summer Games	45	69	65	179
Winter Games	43	37	46	126
Best sports				
Alpine skiing	18	19	18	55
Gymnastics	16	19	13	48
Bobsleigh	9	10	11	30
Rowing	6	8	9	23
Equestrian	4	10	9	23
Shooting	6	6	8	20
Wrestling	4	4	6	14
Cycling	3	6	4	13
Snowboarding	5	1	3	9
Fencing	1	4	3	8

Did you know?

Switzerland won Team Gold for Architecture (Design for a modern stadium) at the Stockholm Games of 1912. The art competitions no longer count as official medals.

Swiss athlete with most Olympic medals:

Georges Miez with eight in gymnastics – four gold, three silver and one bronze – between 1924 and 1936.

Youngest Swiss Olympic medal winner:

Hans Bourquin (13 years, 292 days) won rowing gold in Amsterdam, 1928 as the coxswain for the men's coxed pair.

Oldest Swiss Olympic medal winner:

Louis Noverraz (66 years, 158 days) won sailing silver in Mexico City, 1968 as part of a three-man team in the 5.5m class.

Swiss athlete with most Olympic appearances:

Christine Stückelberger with six in equestrian events – 1972, 1976, 1984, 1988, 1996, 2000 – winning one gold, two silver and one bronze.

Did you know?

Switzerland is one of only two countries (Great Britain is the other) to have competed in all 47 modern Olympic Games, although in 1908 and 1912 the Swiss team was just one athlete – Julius Wagner. In fact, Switzerland once boycotted the Games (Melbourne, 1956) over the Soviet invasion of Hungary but the equestrian events had already been held in Stockholm five months earlier, where Switzerland won a team bronze in Equestrian Dressage.

Olympic Gold medal winners

Summer Games

Athens 1896
Louis Zutter   Gymnastics, pommel horse

Paris 1900
Hermann de Portalés   Sailing, 1-2 ton
Emil Kellenberger   Shooting, military rifle 300m
Team Gold   Shooting, military rifle 300m
Konrad Stäheli   Shooting, military rifle kneeling 300m
Team Gold   Shooting, military pistol 50m
Karl Röderer   Shooting, pistol 50m

St Louis 1904
Adolf Spinnler   Gymnastics, combined three events

Antwerp 1920
Team Gold   Rowing, men's coxed fours
Robert Roth   Wrestling, freestyle heavyweight

Paris 1924
Alphonse Gemuseus   Equestrian, jumping
August Güttinger   Gymnastics, parallel bars
Josef Wilhelm   Gymnastics, pommel horse
Team Gold   Rowing, men's coxed fours
Team Gold   Rowing, men's coxed pairs
Fritz Hagmann   Wrestling, freestyle middleweight
Herman Gehri   Wrestling, freestyle welterweight

Amsterdam 1928
Georges Miez   Gymnastics, all-round
Georges Miez   Gymnastics, horizontal bar
Team Gold   Gymnastics, men's
Hermann Hänggi   Gymnastics, pommel horse
Eugen Mack   Gymnastics, vault
Team Gold   Rowing, men's coxed pairs
Ernst Kyburz   Wrestling, freestyle middleweight

Berlin 1936
Georges Miez   Gymnastics, floor

Olympic Gold medal winners

London 1948
Hans Moser	Equestrian, dressage
Josef Stalder	Gymnastics, horizontal bar
Michael Reusch	Gymnastics, parallel bars
Karl Frei	Gymnastics, rings
Emil Grünig	Shooting, free rifle 300m

Helsinki 1952
Jack Günthard	Gymnastics, horizontal bar
Hans Eugster	Gymnastics, parallel bars

Tokyo 1964
Henri Chammartin	Equestrian, dressage

Montreal 1976
Christine Stückelberger	Equestrian, dressage

Moscow 1980
Robert Dill-Bundi	Cycling, 4000m individual pursuit
Jürg Röthlisberger	Judo, middleweight

Barcelona 1992
Marc Rosset	Tennis, men's singles

Atlanta 1996
Pascal Richard	Cycling, individual road race
Donghua Li	Gymnastics, pommel horse
Markus Gier	Rowing, lightweight double sculls
& Michael Gier	
Xeno Müller	Rowing, single sculls

Sydney 2000
Brigitte McMahon	Triathlon

Athens 2004
Marcel Fischer	Fencing, individual epée

Beijing 2008
Fabian Cancellara	Cycling, time trial
Roger Federer	Tennis, men's doubles
& Stanislas Wawrinka	

Winter Games

Chamonix 1924
Team Gold   Bobsleigh, four-man

Garmisch-Partenkirchen 1936
Team Gold   Bobsleigh, four-man

St Moritz 1948
Edy Reinalter   Alpine skiing, men's slalom
Hedy Schlunegger   Alpine skiing, women's downhill
Felix Endrich   Bobsleigh, two-man
& Fritz Waller

Cortina d'Ampezzo 1956
Madeline Berthod   Alpine skiing, women's downhill
Renée Colliard   Alpine skiing, women's slalom
Team Gold   Bobsleigh, four-man

Squaw Valley 1960
Roger Staub   Alpine skiing, men's giant slalom
Yvonne Rüegg   Alpine skiing, women's giant slalom

Sapporo 1972
Bernhard Russi   Alpine skiing, men's downhill
Marie-Theres Nadig   Alpine skiing, women's downhill
Marie-Theres Nadig   Alpine skiing, women's giant slalom
Team Gold   Bobsleigh, four-man

Innsbruck 1976
Heini Hemmi   Alpine skiing, men's giant slalom

Lake Placid 1980
Erich Schärer   Bobsleigh, two-man
& Josef Benz

Sarajevo 1984
Max Julen   Alpine skiing, men's giant slalom
Michela Figini   Alpine skiing, women's downhill

Winter Games

Calgary 1988

Pirmin Zurbriggen	Alpine skiing, men's downhill
Vreni Schneider	Alpine skiing, women's giant slalom
Vreni Schneider	Alpine skiing, women's slalom
Team Gold	Bobsleigh, four-man
Hipployt Kempf	Nordic combined, men's individual

Albertville 1992

Gustav Weder & Donat Acklin	Bobsleigh, two-man

Lillehammer 1994

Vreni Schneider	Alpine skiing, women's slalom
Gustav Weder & Donat Acklin	Bobsleigh, two-man
Andrea Schönbächler	Freestyle skiing, men's aerials

Nagano 1998

Team Gold	Curling, men's
Gian Simmen	Snowboarding, men's halfpipe

Salt Lake City 2002

Simon Ammann	Ski jumping, men's 90m
Simon Ammann	Ski jumping, men's 120m
Philipp Schoch	Snowboarding, men's parallel giant slalom

Torino 2006

Evelyne Leu	Freestyle skiing, women's aerials
Maya Pederson-Bieri	Skeleton, women's
Philipp Schoch	Snowboarding, men's parallel giant slalom
Tanja Frieden	Snowboarding, women's cross
Daniela Meuli	Snowboarding, women's parallel giant slalom

Vancouver 2010

Didier Défago	Alpine skiing, men's downhill
Carlo Janka	Alpine skiing, men's giant slalom
Dario Cologna	Cross-country skiing, men's 15km
Michael Schmid	Freestyle skiing, men's ski cross
Simon Ammann	Ski jumping, men's 90m
Simon Ammann	Ski jumping, men's 120m

Milestones on Swiss Roads

The first...

...motorised Postbus, from Bern to Detligen	1906
...fuel duty, to help pay the federal debt after the First World War	1921
...use of the three-tone horn on mountain Postbus routes	1923
...Swiss traffic survey: 105,000 vehicles or 1 for every 37 people	1929
...uniform traffic rules and signals throughout Switzerland	1932
...traffic lights: in Geneva	1935
...parking meters in Europe: in Basel	1952
...section of motorway: between Lucerne and Horw	1955
...uniform colour for all Postbuses	1959
...motorway service station: on the A1 near Köllikon, AG	1967
...female Postbus driver: Claire Buner on the Jonschil-Uzwil route	1971

The highest ever annual death toll on Swiss roads was 1,773 in 1971.

Did you know?
The last Grand Prix car race to be held in Switzerland was on 22 August 1954 at the Bremgarten track near Bern. It was won by Juan Manuel Fangio of Argentina. Car races were banned in 1958.

The United Nations in Geneva

The UN has its European base in Geneva, where it replaced the old League of Nations. It employs around 8,500 staff.

UN bodies with world headquarters in Geneva

ECE	Economic Commission for Europe
IBE	International Bureau of Education
ICC	International Computing Centre
ILO	International Labour Organisation
ISDR	International Strategy for Disaster Reduction
ITC	International Trade Centre
ITU	International Telecommunication Union
JIU	Joint Inspection Unit
NGLS	UN Non-Governmental Liaison Service
OCHA	Office for Coordination of Human Affairs
UNAIDS	Joint UN Programme in HIV / AIDS
UNCC	UN Compensation Commission
UNCTAD	UN Conference on Trade and Development
UNHCHR	Office of UN High Commissioner for Human Rights
UNHCR	Office of UN High Commissioner for Refugees
UNIDIR	UN Institute for Disarmament Research
UNITAR	UN Institute for Training and Research
UNOG	UN Office at Geneva
UNRISD	UN Research Institute for Social Development
WHO	World Health Organisation
WIPO	World Intellectual Property Organisation
WMO	World Meteorological Organisation
WTO	World Trade Organisation

Did you know?
Geneva is also home to over 250 other international bodies and non-governmental organizations (NGOs), such as the International Committee of the Red Cross, CERN (the European Organisation for Nuclear Research), and the World Organisation of the Scout Movement.

Heidi on Film

Many actresses have
played the title role
in filmed versions
of Heidi, either in
English or German.

1920	English	Madge Evans
1937	English	Shirley Temple
1952 / 1954 / 1955	German	Elsbeth Sigmund
1953 / 1954	English	Julia Lockwood
1958	English	Sandy Descher
1959	English	Sarah O'Connor
1965	German	Eva Maria Singhammer
1968	English	Jennifer Edwards
1974	English	Emma Blake
1978	German	Katia Polletin
1978	English	Katy Kurtzman
1990	English	Juliette Caton
1993	English	Noley Thornton
2001	German	Cornelia Gröschel
2005	English	Emma Bolger

Did you know?

Elsbeth Sigmund was born in Winterthur in 1942, making her
the only real Swiss Heidi. Cornelia Gröschel is German and,
almost unthinkable for many Swiss, Katia Polletin and Eva Maria
Singhammer both Austrian – rather like having an American play
Harry Potter.

Ten Largest Lakes

The total area of all lakes in Switzerland is 1422.4 km², or a little larger than Canton Aargau. In comparison, Lake Superior in the US is 57 times as big as t he combined total of Swiss lakes (and twice as big as the whole of Switzerland).

	Area (km²)
Lake Neuchâtel	215.2
Lake Lucerne	113.7
Lake Zurich	88.2
Lake Thun	47.7
Lake Biel	39.5
Lake Zug	38.4
Lake Brienz	29.8
Lake Walen	24.2
Lake Murten	22.8
Lake Sempach	14.4

Lakes shared with other countries

	Total area, km²	Swiss part, km²
Lake Geneva (with France)	580	345.3
Lake Constance (with Austria & Germany)	536	172.9
Lago Maggiore (with Italy)	210.2	40.5
Lago di Lugano (with Italy)	48.7	30.0

Did you know?

Excluding the lakes shared with neighbouring countries, then Lake Brienz is the deepest (261m) and Lake Neuchâtel has the largest volume of water (14,170 million m³). In comparison, Lake Murten is only 46 metres deep and contains just 600 million m³.

Important Swiss battles

Switzerland wasn't always neutral so has fought in more than a few crucial battles.

Morgarten (SZ)	15 Nov 1315	Swiss defeat Habsburgs
Laupen (BE)	21 Jun 1339	Bern defeats Fribourg
Sempach (LU)	9 Jul 1386	Swiss defeat Habsburgs
Näfels (GL)	9 Apr 1388	Swiss defeat Habsburgs
St Jakob an der Birs (BL)	26 Aug 1444	France defeats the Swiss
Grandson (VD)	2 Mar 1476	Swiss defeat Burgundy
Murten (FR)	22 Jun 1476	Swiss defeat Burgundy
Nancy (France)	5 Jan 1477	Swiss defeat Burgundy
Calven (Italy)	22 May 1499	Graubünden defeats Habsburgs
Dornach (SO)	22 Jul 1499	Swiss defeat Holy Roman Empire
Marignano (Italy)	13-14 Sept 1515	France defeats the Swiss
Kappel am Albis (ZH)	11 Oct 1531	Catholic cantons defeat Zurich
Grauholz (BE)	3 Mar 1798	France defeats Bern
Zurich	25-26 Sept 1799	France defeats Russia & Austria
Gisikon (LU)	23 Nov 1847	Federal forces defeat Sonderbund

Did you know?
The legendary hero of the Battle of Sempach was Arnold Winkelried from Nidwalden. He sacrificed himself to give the Swiss forces the chance to break through the Habsburg lines. Sadly there is no evidence to prove it.

Swiss Football Championships

The winner of the first championship (1897/8 season) was
Grasshopper Club Zurich.

Most titles:

27 Grasshopper Club Zurich

17 Servette FC

15 FC Basel

12 FC Zurich

11 BSC Young Boys

 7 Lausanne-Sports

 3 FC Aarau, FC La Chaux-de-Fonds, FC Lugano, FC Winterthur

 2 Neuchâtel Xamax, FC Sion, FC St Gallen

 1 AC Bellinzona, Anglo-American FC Zurich, Cantonal Neuchâtel
    FC, FC Biel/Bienne, FC Étoile-Sporting,
    FC Luzern, SC Brühl St Gallen

Four titles in a row: 1957-60 BSC Young Boys

Winners & runners-up since 2000:

Year	Winner	Runner-up
2000	FC St Gallen	Lausanne-Sports
2001	Grasshopper Club	FC Lugano
2002	FC Basel	Grasshopper Club Zurich
2003	Grasshopper Club	FC Basel
2004	FC Basel	BSC Young Boys
2005	FC Basel	FC Thun
2006	FC Zurich	FC Basel
2007	FC Zurich	FC Basel
2008	FC Basel	BSC Young Boys
2009	FC Zurich	BSC Young Boys
2010	FC Basel	BSC Young Boys
2011	FC Basel	FC Zurich
2012	FC Basel	FC Luzern

The Roof of Europe

About 23% of Switzerland sits at over 2000m, and around 2% is over 4000m, with 48 named peaks.

Dufourspitze*	4634m	Strahlhorn	4190m
Nordend	4609m	Combin de Valsorey	4184m
Zumsteinspitze	4563m	Dent d'Hérens	4171m
Signalkuppe	4554m	Breithorn Westgipfel	4165m
Dom	4545m	Breithorn Mittelgipfel	4159m
Liskamm Ost	4527m	Jungfrau	4158m
Weisshorn	4506m	Bishorn	4153m
Täschhorn	4491m	Combin de la Tsessette	4141m
Liskamm West	4479m	Breithorn Ostgipfel	4139m
Matterhorn	4478m	Mönch	4107m
Parrotspitze	4432m	Breithornzwillinge	4106m
Dent Blanche	4357m	Pollux	4092m
Ludwigshöhe	4341m	Schreckhorn	4078m
Nadelhorn	4327m	Roccia Nera	4075m
Combin de Grafeneire	4314m	Ober Gabelhorn	4063m

*also known as Monte Rosa

Lenzspitze	4294m	Piz Bernina	4049m
Finsteraarhorn	4274m	Gross Fiescherhorn	4049m
Stecknadelhorn	4241m	Gross Grünhorn	4044m
Castor	4228m	Lauteraarhorn	4042m
Zinalrothorn	4221m	Dirruhorn	4035m
Hohberghorn	4219m	Allalinhorn	4027m
Alphubel	4206m	Hinter Fiescherhorn	4025m
Rimpfischhorn	4199m	Weissmies	4023m
Aletschhorn	4193m	Lagginhorn	4010m

Ten other famous mountains.

Eiger	3970m	Titlis	3238m
Piz Palü	3901m	Schilthorn	2970m
Wetterhorn	3692m	Säntis	2502m
Dammastock	3630m	Pilatus	2132m
Piz Buin	3312m	Rigi	1797m

RIMPFISCHHORN   STRAHLHORN

How to Play Hornussen

A traditional Swiss game of cricket-meets-golf, played between two teams of 16 – 18 people. One side launches a small puck into the air while the other tries to bat it down with giant paddles. Then they swap over and the fielders become the puck-flickers. After two rounds each, the game is over.

The equipment

- The Ries, or playing field, is 200 metres long and 8 metres (at the start) to 15 metres (at the end) wide. It is divided into 20 Zieli, or bands, each 10 metres deep and worth one point. The striker stands 100 meters back from the first Zieli, separated from the Ries by a no-go area, or Eschenlatte.

- The Hornuss, or puck, weighs 78g and was originally made from stone, bone or wood but now is carbon fibre. It sits on the tip of a curved metal ramp, the Bock, waiting to be shot through the air at up to 300km/h.

- The Stecken is the scarily long fibre-glass whip that's used to launch the Hornuss. It can be up to 3 metres long and at its tip is a compressed wooden block, known as the Träf.

- Each fielder has a Schindel, or paddle, usually made from wood and weighing about 4kg. It resembles a giant version of those long-handled boards used to slide pizzas in and out of an oven.

- No player is allowed to be bare-chested (Rule 174).

The game

- The striker swings his Stecken round his body, spins back quickly to slide the Träf along the Bock, hit the Hornuss and catapult it over the Eschenlatte and far into the Ries.

- Fielders standing (unprotected) in the Ries throw their Schindels up into the air to try and bring down the Hornuss, or at least stop it flying too far.

- If the Hornuss lands inside the Ries without having been hit by a Schindel, the fielding team receives a Nummer, or penalty. That's a bad thing.

- When a Hornuss lands inside the Ries, even after interception, the striker gets one point for every Zieli covered, eg if it flies 240 metres, it will land 140 metres inside the Ries, so covering 14 Zieli and scoring 14 points. That's a good thing.

- Each striker gets two hits of the Hornuss per round, with the home side going first. The round is over when all team members have finished striking.

- The winners are the team with the fewest Nummers at the end. If there's a tie, the team with the most points wins.

Glossary

Bock	launching rail
Eschenlatte	100m no-go zone
Hornuss	puck (also called Nouss)
Nummer	penalty
Ries	playing field
Schindel	giant paddle
Stecken	whip
Träf	wooden end of the whip
Zieli	scoring bands

James Bond and Switzerland

Britain's most famous secret agent has many Swiss connections.

- James Bond's mother was Swiss: Monique Delacroix from Canton Vaud
- Ian Fleming, the creator of 007, went to university in Geneva
- The first Bond girl was Honey Ryder in Dr No (1962), played by Ursula Andress from Ostermundigen (BE)
- The 22nd Bond film, Quantum of Solace (2008), was directed by Marc Forster, who is half Swiss half-German and grew up in Davos
- Swiss actor Anatole Taubman played Elvis in Quantum of Solace, and has a line of dialogue in Swiss German: "ja, Mami, es isch scho e chli heiss" or "yes Mum, it's already a bit hot"
- Sir Roger Moore has his winter home in Crans-Montana
- Swiss rapper and actor Carlos Leal played the poker tournament director in Casino Royale (2006)
- David Niven, who played Bond in the spoof Casino Royale (1967), is buried in Chateau-d'Oex cemetery
- Switzerland was used for various Bond locations:
- Goldfinger (1964) – Furka Pass, Furka Strasse, Realp, Aurora petrol station (Andermatt), Pilatus aircraft factory (Stans)
- On Her Majesty's Secret Service (1969) – Bern (Schweizerhof Hotel, Bahnhofplatz, Heiliggeist Kirche, Nydegg bridge), Lauterburnnen, Mürren, Grindelwald, Winteregg, Piz Gloria Schilthorn
- Goldeneye (1995) – Verzasca Dam (Ticino)

Did you know?

Bernese actress Ursula Andress became an icon thanks to a white bikini. Her Swiss accent was so strong that in Dr No her voice was dubbed over. All the same her role as Honey Ryder earned her $10,000 and a Golden Globe in 1964 for Most Promising Female Newcomer.

Happy Swiss Birthday

Switzerland celebrates its national day on 1 August, although none of its most famous children shares that birthday.

Ursula Andress	actress	19 March 1936
Sepp Blatter	football boss	10 March 1936
DJ Bobo	pop star	5 January 1968
Alain de Botton	author, philosopher	20 December 1969
Louis Chevrolet	car maker	25 December 1878
Le Corbusier	architect	6 October 1857
Didier Cuche	skier	16 August 1974
Henri Dunant	Red Cross founder	8 May 1828
Leonhard Euler	mathematician	15 April 1707
Roger Federer	tennis player	8 August 1981
Max Frisch	author	15 May 1911
Alberto Giacometti	sculptor	10 October 1901
Ferdinand Hodler	artist	14 March 1853
Carl Jung	psychiatrist	20 July 1875
Anton Mosimann	chef	22 February 1947
Heinrich Pestalozzi	educator	12 January 1746
Pingu	cartoon character	7 March 1990
Cäsar Ritz	hotelier	23 February 1850
Jean-Jacques Rousseau	philosopher	28 June 1712
Johanna Spyri	author	12 June 1827
Ulrich Zwingli	religious reformer	1 January 1484

Did you know?

St Nicholas of Flüe is the patron saint of Switzerland. He was born on 21 March 1417 in Sachseln (OW) and was married with 10 children. He was a soldier, farmer and cantonal judge before becoming a hermit, and his intervention in 1481 prevented a civil war. He apparently survived 19 (or maybe 20) years without any food or water, and eventually died on his 70th birthday. He was canonised by Pope Pius XII in 1947.

Wakker Prize Winners

The Wakker Prize of 20,000 francs is awarded annually by the Swiss Heritage Society to communities or organisations for achievements in architecture. The first prize went to Stein am Rhein in 1972.

Winners since 2000

2000 Geneva (GE): For its work on upgrading the public spaces along the Rhone and especially the project 'Le Fil du Rhone'.

2001 Uster (ZH): For creating its own identity in an anonymous agglomeration, integrating contemporary archictecture and old buildings.

2002 Turgi (AG): For showing how a small community can develop high-quality housing with good planning and contemporary design.

2003 Sursee (LU): For preserving its historic core while upgrading the surrounding urban space after years of neglect.

2004 Biel/Bienne (BE): For restoring its unique architectural heritage from the 20th century and creating new public spaces.

2005 SBB (Swiss Federal Railways): For exemplary commitment to architectural culture, being a good role model and respecting architectural heritage.

2006 Delémont (JU): For its clear planning strategy, producing considerate urban development and less rigid rules.

2007 Altdorf (UR): For its clear planning, sustainable management of the townscape and amazing variety of new buildings.

2008 Grenchen (SO): For its enhancement of public spaces, careful city development and respect for the numerous postwar buildings.

1972 Stein am Rhein (SH)	1986 Diemtigen (BE)	2000 Genf (GE)
1973 Saint-Prex (VD)	1987 Bischofszell ((TG)	2001 Uster (ZH)
1974 Wiedlisbach (BE)	1988 Porrentruy (JU)	2002 Turgi (AG)
1975 Guarda (GR)	1989 Winterthur (ZH)	2003 Sursee (LU)
1976 Grüningen (ZH)	1990 Montreux (VD)	2004 Biel/Bienne (BE)
1977 Gais (AR)	1991 Cham (ZG)	2005 SBB
1978 Dardagny (GE)	1992 St. Gallen (SG)	2006 Delémont (JU)
1979 Ernen (VS)	1993 Monte Carasso (TI)	2007 Altdorf (UR)
1980 Solothurn (SO)	1994 La Chaux-de-Fonds (NE)	2008 Grenchen (SO)
1981 Elm (GL)	1995 Splügen (GR)	2009 Yverdon-les-Bains (VD)
1982 Avegno (TI)	1996 Basel (BS)	2010 Fläsch (GR)
1983 Muttenz (BL)	1997 Bern (BE)	2011 Lausanne West (VD)
1984 Wil SG (SG)	1998 Vrin (GR)	2012 Köniz (BE)
1985 Laufenburg (AG)	1999 Hauptwil-Gottshaus (TG)	

2009 Yverdon-les-Bains (VD): For its treatment of public spaces, cross-community co-operation and noticeable creative desire.

2010 Fläsch (GR): For its innovative town planning, preserving the characteristic wine and fruit gardens in the town centre.

2011 Lausanne West: For the co-ordinated approach of nine communities to planning and creating a common identity.

2012 Köniz (BE): For its exemplary residential developments, which are a model for suburban communities with clear demarcations between rural and urban.

Did you know?
The prize was made possible by the bequest of Geneva business-man Henri-Louis Wakker. He died on 17 March 1972, one day before his 97th birthday.

Swiss Hit Parade

A weekly music chart since 1968

Singles with most weeks on the chart

Title	Artist	Weeks	Peak (weeks)
Ein Stern	D J Ötzi & Nik P.	118	2 (2)
Chasing Cars	Snow Patrol	105	4 (1)
Bring en hei	Baschi	100	1 (6)
Hung Up	Madonna	99	1 (7)
You're Beautiful	James Blunt	97	2 (3)
This is the Life	Amy McDonald	94	2 (3)
Ewigi Liäbi	Mash	91	9 (1)
Apologize	Timbaland Presents One Republic	89	1 (6)
Rehab	Amy Winehouse	88	11 (1)
Rise Up	Yves Larock	88	16 (1)

Artists with most weeks on the singles chart

Artist	Weeks	Singles
Madonna	957	63
Rihanna	693	25
Michael Jackson	621	48
David Guetta	561	23
P!nk	555	23
Nelly Furtado	516	17
Britney Spears	511	27
DJ Bobo	487	31
Eminem	484	25
Black Eyed Peas	480	16

Singles with most weeks at Number 1

Title	Artist	Weeks	Year
Whenever Wherever	Shakira	17	2002
I Do it for You	Bryan Adams	16	1991
My Heart Will Go On	Céline Dion	15	1998
Dolannes-Melodie	Jean-Claude Dorelly	14	1975-6
Rivers of Babylon	Boney M	14	1978
Lambada	Kaoma	14	1989
Rhythm is a Dancer	Snap!	14	1992
What's Up?	4 Non Blondes	14	1993
Dragostea din tei	O-Zone	14	2004

Most successful single of each year

Year	Title	Artist	Weeks at No 1
1968	Monja	Roland W.5	
1969	Eloise	Barry Ryan	4
1970	A Song of Joy	Miguel Rios	7
1971	Chirpy Chirpy Cheep Cheep	Middle of the Road	9
1972	Popcorn	Hot Butter	10
1973	Goodbye my Love, Goodbye	Demis Roussos	12
1974	Seasons in the Sun	Terry Jacks	3
1975	Torneró	I Santo California	6
1976	Fernando	Abba	11
1977	Living Next Door to Alice	Smokie	7
1978	Rivers of Babylon	Boney M	14
1979	YMCA	Village People	8
1980	Another Brick in the Wall (Part II)	Pink Floyd	11

Most successful single of each year

Year	Title	Artist	Weeks at No 1
1981	Stars on 45	Stars on 45	6
1982	Words	F.R. David	6
1983	Flashdance (What a Feeling)	Irene Cara	4
1984	Self Control	Laura Branigan	8
1985	Live is Life	Opus	2 (4)
1986	Adesso tu	Eros Ramazzotti	1
1987	Voyage Voyage	Desireless	4 (2)
1988	Küss' die Hand, schöne Frau	Erste Allgemeine Verunsicherung	2 (3)
1989	Looking for Freedom	David Hasselhoff	4
1990	Un'estate italiana	Edoardo Bennato & Gianna Nannini	1
1991	Wind of Change	Scorpions	5
1992	It's My Life	Dr Alban	2 (10)
1993	Somebody Dance with Me	D J Bobo	1
1994	Without You	Maariah Carey	10
1995	Have You Ever Really Loved a Woman?	Bryan Adams	2
1996	Macarena	Los del Rio	4
1997	Time to Say Goodbye	Sarah Brightman & Andrea Bocelli	6
1998	My Heart Will Go On	Céline Dion	15
1999	Mambo No 5 (A Little Bit of…)	Lou Bega	11
2000	Freestyler	Bomfunk MCs	10
2001	Can't Get You out of My Head	Kylie Minogue	4
2002	The Ketchup Song (Aserejé)	Las Ketchup	11
2003	Chihuahua	DJ Bobo	10
2004	Dragostea din tei	O-Zone	14
2005	Schnappi, das kleine Krokodil	Schnappi	8

2006	Hips Don't Lie	Shakira featuring Wyclef Jean	7
2007	Ein Stern	D J Ötzi & Nik P	2 (2)
2008	Apologize	Timbaland Presents OneRepublic	6
2009	Poker Face	Lady Gaga	8
2010	Waka Waka (This Time for Africa)	Shakira featuring Freshlyground	4
2011	On the Floor	Jennifer Lopez Featuring Pitbull	5

*where a single didn't reach No 1, the highest chart position is shown, with the number of weeks at that position in brackets.

Albums with most weeks on the chart

Title	Artist	Weeks	Peak
Gold	Abba	265	1 (9)
The Fame	Lady Gaga	140	1 (6)
Back to Black	Amy Winehouse	134	1 (11)
Come Away with Me	Norah Jones	132	2 (1)
Piece by Piece	Katie Melua	129	3 (1)
Californication	Red Hot Chili Peppers	123	3 (2)
Plüsch	Plüsch	118	6 (2)
Clandestino	Manu Chao	115	9 (1)
Uf U Dervo	Gölä	111	1 (9)
This is the Life	Amy McDonald	106	1 (5)

Artists with most weeks on the album chart

Artist	Weeks	Albums
Céline Dion	577	22
Eros Ramazotti	524	17
Madonna	499	22
Michael Jackson	485	19
Gotthard	460	14
Robbie Williams	409	14
DJ Bobo	406	17
Bon Jovi	402	15
Laura Pausini	399	12
U2	398	16

The Ricola Herbs

Ricola herbal drops were first created in the summer of 1940 by Emil Richterich. They contain 13 herbs, all grown in Switzerland, and the drops themselves are made in Laufen (BL).

Burnet	*Pimpinella saxifraga*
Cowslip	*Primula veris*
Elder	*Sambucus nigra*
Horehound	*Marrubium vulgare*
Lady's mantle	*Alchemilla vulgaris*
Mallow	*Malva sylvestris*
Marshmallow	*Alathea officinalis*
Peppermint	*Mentha piperita*
Plantain	*Plantago lanceolata*
Sage	*Salvia officinalis*
Speedwell	*Veronica officinalis*
Thyme	*Thymus vulgaris*
Yarrow	*Achillea millefolium*

Swiss Films on the Big Screen

Over 14.9 million cinema tickets were sold in Switzerland in 2011, roughly two per person; Swiss films made up only 5.4% of those seen. Here are the most successful Swiss films since 1975, with the cumulative audience numbers in Switzerland.

	Audience
1. Die Schweizermacher (1978, Rolf Lyssy) Two inspectors check out potential new Swiss citizens	940,508
2. Achtung, Fertig, Charlie! (2003, Mike Eschmann) "The Swiss answer to American Pie"	560,514
3. Die Herbstzeitlosen (2006, Bettina Oberli) A widow opens a lingerie shop in an Emmental village	559,051
4. Mein Name ist Eugen (2005, Michael Steiner) Boy's-own adventure through Switzerland in the Sixties	542,195
5. Les Petites Fugues (1979, Yves Yersin) One man, his moped, a camera and a farm in Vaud	424,687
6. Grounding (2005, Michael Steiner & Tobias Fueter) The last days of a doomed company: Swissair	370,984
7. Ein Schweizer namens Nötzli (1988, Gustav Ehmck) Unassuming accountant accidentally becomes a success	350,681
8. Ernstfall in Havanna (2002, Sabine Boss) Our (Swiss) man in Havana causes a second Cuban crisis	313,617
9. Höhenfeuer (1985, Fredy-Melchior Murer) Incest and murder on an isolated Alpine farm	253,944
10. Vitus (2006, Fredy-Melchior Murer) Gifted child pianist changes his grandfather's life	243,399

Did you know?

There are 288 cinemas in Switzerland with a total of 106,642 seats. Canton Bern has the most cinemas (57) but Canton Zurich has more seats (18,924). Appenzell Innerrhoden is the only canton without a cinema.

The Seven Federal Departments

Each of the seven federal departments is represented by a Federal Councillor.

DDPS	Federal Department of Defence, Civil Protection and Sports
VBS	Eidgenössisches Departement für Verteidigung, Bevölkerungsschutz und Sport
DDPS	Département fédéral de la défense, de la protection de la population et des sports
DDPS	Dipartimento federale della difesa, della protezione della popolazione e dello sport
DDPS	Departament federal de la defensiun, de la protecziun de la populaziun e dal sport
DETEC	Federal Department of Transport, Communications and Energy
UVEK	Eidgenössisches Departement für Umwelt, Verkehr, Energie und Kommunikation
DETEC	Département fédéral de l'environnement, des transports, de l'énergie et de la communication
DATEC	Dipartimento federale dell'ambiente, dei trasporti, dell'energia e delle comunicazioni
DATEC	Departament federal da l'ambient, dals transports, da l'energia e da la communicaziun
FDEA	Federal Department of Economic Affairs
EVD	Eidgenössisches Volkswirtschaftsdepartement
DFE	Département fédéral de l'économie
DFE	Dipartimento federale dell'economia
DFE	Departament federal da l'economia
FDF	Federal Department of Finance
EFD	Eidgenössisches Finanzdepartement
DFF	Département fédéral des finances
DFF	Dipartimento federaledelle finanze
DFF	Departament federal da finanzas
FDFA	Federal Department of Foreign Affairs
EDA	Eidgenössisches Departement für auswärtige Angelegenheiten

DFAE	Département fédéral des affaires étrangères
DFAE	Dipartimento federale degli affari esteri
DFAE	Departament federal dals affars externs

FDHA	Federal Department of Home Affairs
EDI	Eidgenössisches Departement des Innern
DFI	Département fédéral de l'intérieur
DFI	Dipartimento federale dell'interno
DFI	Departament federal da l'intern

FDJP	Federal Department of Justice and Police
EJPD	Eidgenössisches Justiz- und Polizeidepartement
DFJP	Département fédéral de justice et police
DFGP	Dipartimento federale di giustiza e polizia
DFGP	Departament federal da giustiza e polizia

The Federal Chancellors

The Federal Chancellor heads the Federal Chancellery, or civil service. He/she is elected by parliament to serve as the chief of staff to the Federal Council, sitting in on meetings but without a vote, and so is often known as the unofficial 8th Councillor.

Johann Ulrich Schiess	FDP	AR	1848-1881
Gottlieb Ringier	FDP	AG	1881-1909
Hans Schatzmann	FDP	AG	1909-1918
†Adolf von Steiger	FDP	BE	1918-1925
Robert Kaeslin	FDP	AG	1925-1934
Georges Bovet	FDP	NE	1934-1943
Oskar Leimgruber	CVP	AG	1943-1951
Charles Oser	FDP	BS	1951-1967
Karl Huber	CVP	SG	1967-1981
Walter Buser	SP	BL	1981-1991
François Couchepin	FDP	VS	1991-1999
Annemarie Huber-Hotz	FDP	ZG	1999-2007
Corina Casanova	CVP	GR	2007

†Died in office

Rivers of Ice

There are over 1,450 glaciers in Switzerland – including Europe's longest, the Grosser Aletsch. Here are the top twenty, in terms of length.

Glacier		km	historic lengths (km)	
			1985	1850
Grosser Aletsch	VS	22.7	23.6	26.5
Fiescher	VS	14.9	15.2	17.1
Gorner	VS	12.5	13.2	15.9
Unteraar	BE	11.9	12.7	11.9
Corbassière	VS	9.8	10.2	12.9
Oberaletsch	VS	8.8	9.0	10.4
Unterer Grindelwald	BE	8.3	8.3	9.9
Mont Miné	VS	7.9	8.4	10.1
Rhone	VS	7.8	8.0	9.2
Otemma	VS	7.4	8.3	10
Findelen	VS	7.3	8.0	10.4
Zinal	VS	7.0	7.4	9.1
Hüfi	UR	6.7	7.2	9.2
Zmutt	VS	6.7	6.5	8.6
Lang	VS	6.5	6.8	8.6
Oberer Grindelwald	BE	6.6	6.9	7.4
Alpetli (Kanderfirn)	BE	6.5	6.8	9.2
Ferpècle	VS	6.4	6.7	9.3
Morteratsch	GR	6.3	6.8	8.9
Saleina	VS	6.1	6.6	7.8

Did you know?

Since 1850 Swiss glaciers have lost over one third of their surface area and roughly half their density. It is estimated that the total volume of water locked into in Swiss glaciers is about 65km^3, or much less than that of Lake Geneva.

Lauberhorn Downhill Winners

The first run in 1930 was won by Christian Rubi (Switzerland) and the record number of wins is six by Karl Molitor (Switzerland) between 1939 and 1947.

Winners since 2000

2000	Josef Strobel	Austria
2001	Race cancelled due to bad weather	
2002	Stephan Eberharter	Austria
2003	Bruno Kernen	Switzerland
2004	Race cancelled due to bad weather	
2005	Michael Walchhofer	Austria
2006	Daron Rhalves	USA
2007	Bode Miller	USA
2008	Bode Miller	USA
2009	Didier Défago	Switzerland
2010	Carlo Janka	Switzerland
2011	Klaus Kröll	Austria
2012	Beat Feuz	Switzerland

Did you know?

At 4,480 metres long, the Lauberhorn is the world's longest downhill ski race. The starting elevation is at 2315m and the finish line in Wengen at 1028m, with the steepest section having a gradient of 42°.

Ice Hockey

About 320 ice hockey clubs play in the National (A and B) and
Regional Leagues.

Oldest clubs in the National Leagues

1905	Genève-Servette HC
1919	HC La Chaux-de-Fonds
1921	HC Davos
1922	HC Lausanne
1930	ZSC Lions
1931	SC Bern
1932	EHC Basel Sharks
1932	GCK Lions
1933	HC Sierre
1934	EHC Olten
1934	Kloten Flyers

Did you know?

The most successful ice hockey club is HC Davos with 30
championship wins, followed by SC Bern with 12 and EHC
Arosa with nine.

Chocolate – a National Industry

In 2011 the Swiss consumed 94,008 tonnes of chocolate, or 11.9kg per person, although that figure includes chocolate bought by tourists and visitors.

Exports
107,051 tonnes of chocolate was exported to 150 countries, with Europe accounting for 63%. In francs, that amounts to 820 million.

Germany	17.0%	Canada	6.7%
UK	13.1%	USA	6%
France	9.2%	Italy	5%

Imports
31,962 tonnes of chocolate was imported, 43% coming from Germany. That accounts for 34% of domestic consumption.

Employment
4,328 people, well over half of them women, are employed across the 18 members of the Association of Swiss Chocolate Manufacturers: Alprose, Barry Callebaut, Bernrain, Camille Bloch, Favarger, Felchlin, Frey, Gysi, Halba, Kraft Schweiz, Läderach, Lindt, Maestrani, Nestlé Cailler, Pfister, Sprüngli, Stella, Villars.

Sales
Total sales in 2011 reached 176,332 tonnes of all types of chocolate, generating an income of 1,690 million Swiss francs

Bars	49.6%
Chocolate confectionery	20.9%
Couverture	17.4%
Mini-formats	6.4%
Festive chocolate	5.0%
Cocoa powder	0.7%

Cantonal Rankings

Only two cantons have the same ranking for both area and population: Canton Bern is 2nd and Nidwalden 22nd in both lists. Canton Geneva has the biggest gap between population (6th) and size (21st), while Uri has the largest difference in reverse – 25th in population against 11th in size.

	Ranking/Population		Ranking/Area (km²)	
Aargau	4	611,466	10	1,403.8
Appenzell AI	26	15,688	25	172.5
Appenzell AR	21	53,017	23	242.9
Basel-Land	11	274,404	18	517.5
Basel-Stadt	15	184,950	26	37.1
Bern	2	979,802	2	5,959.1
Fribourg	10	278,493	8	1,670.8
Geneva	6	457,715	21	282.4
Glarus	23	38,608	17	685.4
Graubünden	14	192,621	1	7,105.2
Jura	20	70,032	14	838.8
Lucerne	7	377,610	9	1,493.5
Neuchâtel	16	172,085	15	803.1
Nidwalden	22	41,024	22	276.1
Obwalden	24	35,585	19	490.6
Schaffhausen	19	76,356	20	298.5
Schwyz	17	146,730	13	908.2
Solothurn	12	255,284	16	790.5
St Gallen	5	478,907	6	2,026.4
Thurgau	13	248,444	12	990.9
Ticino	8	333,753	5	2,812.5
Uri	25	35,422	11	1,076.4
Valais	9	312,684	3	5,224.4
Vaud	3	713,281	4	3,212.1
Zug	18	113,105	24	238.8
Zurich	1	1,373,068	7	1,728.8

Causes of Death in 1900 & 2000

	1900	2000
Aids	0	127
Breast cancer	175	1,337
Diabetes	186	1,558
Diphtheria	981	0
Heart attacks & strokes	10,209	24,910
Liver cirrhosis	393	500
Lung cancer	17	2,825
Measles	809	0
Murder	99	16
Pneumonia & bronchitis	10,809	4,625
Pregnancy & giving birth	523	0
Smallpox	30	0
Suicide	764	1,378
Syphilis	143	0
Traffic accidents	247	655
Tuberculosis	9,037	33
Tumours & cancer	4,418	15,978
Typhoid	220	0
Whooping cough	695	0
Unknown (no doctor called)	2,628	0
Total	63,606	62,528

Life expectancy (years)

	1900	2000
Men	45.69	77.22
Women	48.47	82.82

Did you know?

There are 1,332 people over the age of 100 in Switzerland – only 218 are men.

Car Ownership

Many rental cars in Switzerland have an AI number plate, even if rented in Bern or Basel. Big car-hire companies such as Avis, Hertz and Sixt have their fleets registered in Appenzell Innerrhoden (AI), which may explain the unusually high number of cars in such a small place.

12 towns with highest number of cars per 1000 people:			12 towns with lowest number of cars per 1000 people:		
Appenzell	AI	949	Bern	BE	409
Opfikon	ZH	762	Kriens	LU	408
Schlieren	ZH	735	Geneva	GE	404
St Moritz	GR	673	Winterthur	ZH	398
Freienbach	SZ	672	Vevey	VD	393
Sursee	LU	656	Ostermundigen	BE	396
Zug	ZG	636	Lausanne	VD	393
Carouge	GE	633	Riehen	BS	386
Chiasso	TI	615	Horw	LU	383
Frauenfeld	TG	612	Biel	BE	381
Cham	ZG	600	Zurich	ZH	373
Sierre	VS	600	Basel	BS	336

Switzerland: 515 (national average)

Did you know?

From 1900 to 1925 cars were forbidden in Graubünden.

Swiss Person of the Year

The 'Schweizer/-in des Jahres' award began in 2002 and is decided by an annual public vote.

2002	Dr Beat Richner	Hospital founder in Cambodia
2003	Roger Federer	Tennis champion
2004	Lotti Latrous	Humanitarian
2005	Peter Sauber	Formula 1 boss
2006	Köbi Kuhn	National football coach
2007	Jörg Aberhalden	Schwinger champion
2008	Eveline Widmer Schlumpf	Federal Councillor
2009	René Prêtre	Heart surgeon
2010	Marianne Kaufmann & Rolf Maibach	Hospital workers in Haiti
2011	Didier Cuche	Champion skier

Most Common Street Names

There are 132,525 streets in the database of the Swiss online telephone book. These are the 20 most common:

1,460	Dorfstrasse	472	Rosenweg
1,370	Hauptstrasse	453	Oberdorf
1,098	Bahnhofstrasse	449	Gartenstrasse
652	Schulstrasse	417	Haldenstrasse
647	Birkenweg	407	Höhenweg
602	Kirchweg	406	Kirchgasse
594	Oberdorfstrasse	396	Feldstrasse
544	Industriestrasse	394	Unterdorfstrasse
529	Schulhausstrasse	374	Mattenweg
476	Bergstrasse	366	Poststrasse

Swiss Dog Breeds

There are seven breeds officially recognised as being Swiss by the International Canine Federation.

Appenzell Cattle Dog

Bernese Mountain Dog

Entlebuch Cattle Dog

Great Swiss Mountain Dog

St Bernard

Smaller Swiss Hounds

Swiss Hounds

Did you know?

The St Bernard is the Swiss national dog, with the most famous example being Barry. Born in 1800, he had rescued over 40 people from the snow and fog before he retired in 1812. After his death in 1814 he was stuffed and now stands in Bern's Natural History Museum.

The Daily Swiss Diet

What does an average person in Switzerland eat every day? Investigating the daily energy source from different food groups shows that the Swiss are in the global Top Ten when it comes to fat, sugar, cheese, pork (all those sausages) and honey.

Food	Amount	World ranking	World ave.
Energy	3,421 cal	19th (after Hungary)	2,778 cal
Fat	154g	7th (after Italy)	79g
Protein	92g	=42nd (same as Japan)	77g

Daily energy source (kcal)

Food	kcal	World ranking	World ave.
Wheat	628	=83rd (same as Spain)	533
Sugar	535	3rd (after Trinidad)	193
Pork	344	4th (after Luxembourg)	117
Milk	194	=44th (same as Colombia)	79
Animal fat	192	=17th (same as Sweden)	61
Cheese	176	=8th (same as Austria)	25
Potatoes	80	58th (after Luxembourg)	60
Beef	58	=51st (same as Venezuela)	40
Rice	54	=121st (same as Lesotho)	533
Poultry	49	=87th (same as South Korea)	48
Eggs	39	=33rd (same as UK)	33
Maize	16	=136th (same as New Zealand)	138
Pulses	16	=138th (same as Russia)	58
Honey	10	=8th (same as Austria)	2

Ten Longest Rivers

The total length of all flowing water in Switzerland is 61,000km, equivalent to one and a half times round the equator.

	km	Direction	Outflow
Rhine	375*	North	North Sea
Aare	295	North	River Rhine
Rhône	264*	South	Mediterranean Sea
Reuss	158	North	River Aare
Linth-Limmat	140	North	River Aare
Saane/Sarine	128.5	North	River Aare
Thur	125	North	River Rhine
Inn/En	104*	East	River Danube
Ticino	91	South	River Po
Broye	86	North	Lake Neuchâtel

*Swiss section

❧❦ ✚ ❧❦ ❧❦ ✚ ❧❦

Islands in Switzerland

From the Swiss border at Chiasso to the nearest stretch of coastline is 159km, but even a landlocked country has islands.

Brissago islands, Lago Maggiore (TI)
Heidsee islands, Heidsee (GR)
Ile de la Harpe, Lake Geneva (VD)
Länggrien, River Aare (SO)
Lützelau, Lake Zurich (SZ)
Pont-en-Ogoz, Lake Gruyère (FR)
Rheinau Abbey, River Rhine (ZH)
Schnäggen, Lake Brienz (BE)
Schnittlauch Island, Lake Walen (SG)
Schwanau, Lauerzersee (SZ)
Ufenau, Lake Zurich (SZ)
Werdinsel, River Limmat (ZH)

And the Swiss Winner is...

The first ever Academy Award (or Oscar) for Best Actor was won in 1929 by Emil Jannings, a German actor born in Rorschach (SG). He later starred opposite Marlene Dietrich in The Blue Angel.

Best Writing, Original Screenplay

| 1945 | Marie-Louise | Richard Schweizer |

Best Writing, Motion Picture Story

| 1948 | The Search | Richard Schweizer & David Wechsler |

Best Documentary

1962	Le ciel et la Boue	Arthur Cohn*
1991	American Dream	Arthur Cohn*
2000	One Day in September	Arthur Cohn*

Best Visual Effects

| 1980 | Alien | H R Giger |

Best Foreign Language Film

| 1984 | Dangerous Moves (La diagonale du fou) |
| 1990 | Journey of Hope (Reise der Hoffnung) |

*Arthur Cohn has won a total of six Oscars, as he was the producer of three films that won the Best Foreign Language Film: The Garden of the Finzi-Continis (Italy, 1972), Black and White in Color (Ivory Coast, 1977), Dangerous Moves (Switzerland, 1984).

Did you know?

Renée Zellweger, who won the Best Supporting Actress Oscar in 2004 for the film Cold Mountain, is half-Swiss and half-Norwegian. Her father was born in Au (SG) but emigrated after the Second World War.

The Main Political Parties

There are eleven political parties represented in the National Council (NC) and Council of States (CS) in the Federal Parliament.

SVP
Schweizerische Volkspartei (Swiss People's Party). Founded 1971, NC: 54 seats, CS: 5 seats. Right-wing collection of nationalists, farmers, xenophobes and millionaires.

SP
Sozialdemokratische Partei (Social Democratic Party). Founded 1888, NC: 46 seats, CS: 11 seats. Eternal idealists who think Switzerland could be a better place with more taxes.

FDP
Freisinnig-Demokratische Partei (Free Democratic Party). (Officially known as FDP. Die Liberalen after merging with the Liberal Party in 2009.) Founded 1894, NC: 30 seats, CS: 11 seats. The Mrs Thatcher of Swiss politics: once important now fading into insignificance.

CVP
Christlichdemokratische Volkspartei (Christian Democratic Party). Founded 1912, NC: 28 seats, CS: 13 seats. Somewhere in the centre, trying to be all things to everyone but pleasing few.

Die Grünen (Green Party)
Founded 1983, NC: 15 seats, CS: 2 seats. Worthy ecologists saving the world one vote at a time; it could take a while.

GLP
Grünliberale Partei (Green Liberal Party). Founded 2007, NC: 12 seats, CS: 2 seats. They're green and they're liberal. Rather like Shrek with a conscience, only cuter.

BDP

Bürgerlich-Demokratische Partei (Conservative Democratic Party). Founded 2008, NC: 9 seats, CS: 1 seat. SVP-lite with compassionate conservatism replacing strident intolerance.

EVP

Evangelische Volkspartei Partei (Evangelical People's Party). Founded 1919, NC: 2 seats. Protestants who swing left for tax & immigration but right for abortion & gay rights.

CSP

Christlich-soziale Partei (Christian Social Party). Founded 1997, NC: 1 seat. Not a vicar's tea-party but lefty liberals who want to save the environment and tax the rich.

Lega dei Ticinesi (Ticino League)

Founded 1991, NC: 1 seat. Italian-speaking protest party that's anti-EU, anti-Bern and anti-immigrant.

MCG

Mouvement Citoyens Genevois (Geneva Citizen's Movement). Founded 2005, NC: 1 seat. Populist group that claims to be neither left nor right just Genevan.

Did you know?

Party names in the four national languages are generally direct translations of each other, with the corresponding initials. There are two main exceptions: in French and Italian the SVP is known as UDC (Union démocratique du centre and Unione Democratico del Centro), while the FDP is the PLR (Parti libéral-radical and Partito Liberale Radicale).

A Year of Festivals

There are probably enough festivals across the towns, villages and regions of Switzerland to fill a whole book. Here are some of the main traditional ones and most are depicted on the map inside the front cover:

January
Silvesterchläuse, Urnäsch (AR): Masked men in elaborate costumes celebrate the old New Year's Eve.

Vogel Gryff, Basel: A griffin, a lion and a wildman of the woods dance through Klein Basel.

Carnival time (February-March)
Chienbäse, Liestal (BL): Procession of flaming carriages and torches through the old town.

Fasnacht, Lucerne: The largest Catholic carnival begins on 'schmutziger Donnerstag' just before Lent.

Fasnacht, Basel: The 'three most beautiful days', starting with Morgestraich at 4am Monday morning.

Tschäggättä, Lötschental (VS): Huge hairy beasts with scary carved faces roam around the villages.

March
Chalandamarz, Graubünden: Small children ringing giant cowbells to scare away the evil spirits of winter.

Good Friday
Les Pleureuses, Romont (FR): 20 wailing women veiled in black mark the Passion and Crucifixion of Christ.

April
Sechseläuten, Zurich: The start of spring with the burning of the Böögg, or giant snowman.

May
Combat de Reines, Aproz (VS): Final of the Hérens cow fighting competition to decide the 'queen of queens'.

Maibär, Bad Ragaz (SG): The end of winter with a giant flower-and-foliage 'bear' sacrificed for spring.

May-June
Herrgottstag, Düdingen (FR) & Appenzell: Procession with military guards and women in elaborate dresses for Corpus Christi.

July
Alphorn Festival, Nendaz (VS): Annual competition with over 100 players and folkore festivities on the side.

August
Swiss National Day, all over the country: Grilling cervelat speared onto sticks and watching the fireworks.

September
Chästeilet, Hasliberg (BE): The division of that summer's cheese between the dairy farmers.

Fête des vendanges, Neuchâtel: Costumes, bands and parades to celebrate the successful wine harvest.

Knabenschiessen, Zurich: Shooting competition for teenagers and a funfair for everyone.

September-October
Alpabfahrt/Désalpe, various Alpine places: When the cows come home from their summer holidays in the mountains.

La Bénichon, Canton Fribourg: Harvest festival meets gourmet feast of eating and drinking.

October
Aelplerchibli, Nidwalden & Obwalden: Communal eating, dancing and flag-throwing to mark the end of summer.

Castagnata, Ascona (TI): Chestnuts galore: over 2000kg roasted or in jams, breads and cakes.

November
Gansabhauet, Sursee (LU): A form of pin-the-tail-on-the-donkey using a sword, a dead goose and a sun mask.

Rüeblimärt, Aarau (AG): In celebration of Aargau's signature vegetable – the carrot.

Zibelemärit, Bern: Everything you can possibly do to or with an onion.

December
L'Escalade, Geneva: The victory over the Savoyards commemorated with chocolate cauldrons.

Klausjagen, Küssnacht am Rigi (LU): Vast paper headresses lit by candles and carried through town.

Silvesterchläuse, Urnäsch (AR): Masked men in elaborate costumes celebrate the new New Year's Eve.

Tallest Buildings

The tallest man-made structure in Switzerland is the Grand Dixence dam (in Valais) at 285m, or more than twice the height of the Great Pyramid of Giza (see also page 171).

		Year
81m	Mobimo Tower, Zurich	2011
85m	Swissôtel, Zurich	1972
88m	Swisscom Tower, Winterthur	1999
88m	Sunrise Tower, Zurich	2004
91m	Cité du Lignon, Vernier (GE)	1971
95m	Hardau 1, Zurich	1978
99.7m	Sulzer Tower, Winterthur	1966
105m	Messeturm, Basel	2003
126m	Prime Tower, Zurich	2011
178m	Roche Tower 1, Basel	2015*
	*expected opening date	

	Highest church spires	Year
82m	Martinskirche, Chur	1889
91.17m	St Maria Magdalena, Alpnach (OW)	1898
97m	Predigerkirche, Zurich	1900
97.56m	St Martin, Malters (LU)	1835
101m	Münster, Bern	1893

Did you know?

Until 2007 the warden lived in an apartment half-way up Bern Münster's tower; she has had to vacate her flat during the long refurbishment but her office – the highest in Bern – is still in use. At least her sleep is no longer disturbed by the largest bell in Switzerland: the Grosse Glocke (or Big Bell) was cast in 1611, is 247 cm in diameter, and weighs 9.5 tonnes.

Weird Place-Names

Apples (VD)	Lax (VS)
Balm (BE)	Misery (FR)
Bullet (VD)	Mission (VS)
Camp (GR)	Missy (VD)
Concise (VD)	Moosegg (BE)
Chants (GR)	Motto (TI)
Egg (SG, SZ & ZH)	Nods (BE)
Elm (GL)	Piano (TI)
First (BE & ZH)	Places (NE)
Font (FR)	Rain (LU)
Fully (VS)	Root (LU)
Gland (VD)	Run (GR)
Grandson (VD)	Sax (SG)
Grub (AR)	Says (GR)
Hard (SG)	Sent (GR)
Horn (TG)	Vex (VS)
Hub (SG, ZH)	Watt (ZH)

Then the ruder ones:

Bossy (GE)	Sex Rouge (VS)
Bitsch (VS)	Sins (AG)
Cunter (GR)	Titlis (BE-OW)
Harder (BE)	Töss (ZH)
Moron (BE)	Wankdorf (BE)
Sex Noir (VS)	Wildhorn (BE-VS)

And the oddest of all:
Ecce Homo in Canton Schwyz.

Italian – the Third Language

Italian is spoken by 6.5% of the population, primarily in the canton of Ticino and some communities in Graubünden. As Italians are the largest group of resident foreigners, the language is also the mother tongue for many people in the Swiss cities north of the Alps.

Towns with largest number of Italian speakers:

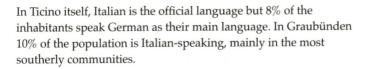

Lugano	54,667	Chiasso	7,737
Zurich	17,524	Geneva	7,320
Bellinzona	17,373	Lausanne	5,113
Locarno	15,153	Winterthur	4,964
Basel	8,814	Bern	4,851

In Ticino itself, Italian is the official language but 8% of the inhabitants speak German as their main language. In Graubünden 10% of the population is Italian-speaking, mainly in the most southerly communities.

Unlike in Italy, where Milano is Milan or Mailand, most place-names in the Italian-speaking part of Switzerland don't change with the language. The big exception is the name of the canton itself. It is Ticino in Italian (and English) but Tessin in the other three languages

Did you know?
In terms of area Ticino is the fifth biggest canton – at 2,812.5km^2 it is marginally larger than Luxembourg – while its population (333,753) is bigger than Iceland's.

The Federal Charter

1291 IN THE NAME OF GOD – AMEN. Honor and the public weal are promoted when leagues are concluded for the proper establishment of quiet and peace. Therefore, know all men, that the people of the valley of Uri, the democracy of the valley of Schwyz, and the community of the Lower Valley of Unterwalden, seeing the malice of the age, in order that they may better defend themselves, and their own, and better preserve them in proper condition, have promised in good faith to assist each other with aid, with every counsel and every favor, with person and goods, within the valley and without, with might and main, against one and all, who may inflict upon any one of them any violence, molestation or injury, or may plot any evil against their persons or goods. And in every case each community has promised to succour the other when necessary, at its own expense, as far as needed in order to withstand the attacks of evil-doers, and to avenge injuries; to this end they have sworn a solemn oath to keep this without guile, and to renew by these presents the ancient form of the league, also confirmed by an oath. Yet in such a manner that every man, according to his rank, shall obey and serve his overlord as it behooves him. We have also vowed, decreed and ordained in common council and by unanimous consent, that we will accept or receive no judge in the aforesaid valleys, who shall have obtained his office for any price, or for money in any way whatever, or one who shall not be a native or a resident with us. But if dissension shall arise between any of the Eidgenossen (confederates; Eid = oath, Genosse = fellow, comrade), the most prudent amongst the confederates shall come forth to settle the difficulty between the parties, as shall seem right to them; and whichever party rejects their verdict shall be held an adversary by the other confederates. Furthermore, it has been established between them that he who deliberately kills another without provocation, shall, if caught, lose his life, as his wicked guilt requires, unless he be able to prove his innocence of said crime; and if per chance he escape, let him never return. Those who conceal and protect said criminal shall be banished from the valley, until they be expressly recalled by the confederates. But if any one of the confederates, by day, or in the silence of the night, shall maliciously injure another by fire, he shall never again be considered a fellow-countryman. If any man protect and defend the said evil-doer, he shall render satisfaction to the one who has suffered damage. Furthermore, if any one of the confederates shall spoil another of his goods, or injure him in any way, the goods of the guilty one, if recovered within the valleys, shall be seized in order to pay damages to the injured person, according to justice. Furthermore, no man shall seize another's goods for debt, unless he be evidently his debtor or surety, and this shall only be done with the special permission of his judge. Moreover, every man shall obey his judge, and if necessary, must himself indicate the judge in the valley, before whom he ought properly to appear. And if any one rebels against a verdict, and, in consequence of his obstinacy, any one of the confederates is injured, all the confederates are bound to compel the culprit to give satisfaction. But if war or discord arise amongst any of the confederates and one party of the disputants refuse to accept the verdict of the judge or to give satisfaction, the confederates are bound to defend the other party. The above-written statutes, decreed for the common welfare and benefit, shall endure forever, God willing. In testimony of which, at the request of the aforesaid parties, the present charter has been drawn up and confirmed with the seals of the aforesaid three communities and valleys.

So done in the year of the Lord 1291 at the beginning of the month of August.

Did you know?

It's not entirely clear who stood in Rütli meadow that August day but the story goes that it was Walter Fürst from Canton Uri, Werner Stauffacher from Canton Schwyz, and Arnold von Melchtal from Canton Unterwalden. William Tell was noticeable by his absence.

Women's Voting Rights – a Chronology

1958	26 June, Riehen (BS): first Swiss community to give women the vote
1959	1 February, cantonal voting rights in Vaud
	29 September, Neuchâtel
1960	6 March, Geneva
1966	26 June, Basel-Stadt
1968	23 June, Basel-Land
1969	19 October, Ticino
1970	12 April, Valais
	25 October, Lucerne
	15 November, Zurich
1971	7 February, voting rights at federal level approved by referendum:
	Yes – 621,109 (65.7%), 15½ cantons
	No – 323,882 (34.3%), 6½ cantons (AI, AR, GL, OW, SG, SZ, TG, UR)
	7 February, Aargau, Fribourg, Schaffhausen and Zug
	2 May, Glarus
	6 June, Solothurn
	12 December, Bern and Thurgau
1972	23 January, St Gallen
	30 January, Uri
	5 March, Graubünden and Schwyz
	30 April, Nidwalden
	24 September, Obwalden
1977	20 March, Jura
1989	30 April, Appenzell Ausserrhoden
1990	27 November, Appenzell Innerrhoden

Solothurn's Magic Number

The number 11 has a special significance in Solothurn. It could be because Solothurn was the 11th canton to join the Confederation, though that only works if you count the half-cantons of Obwalden and Nidwalden separately.

The cathedral

St Ursen cathedral was built in 11 years (1762-73) and has 11 bells, 11 altars and pews in groups of 11. The façade is 33 metres high and the tower 66, while the main staircase is divided into three flights of 11 steps.

The town

There are 11 museums, 11 fountains, 11 chapels, 11 churches, and a clock that only has 11 numbers (the 12 is missing). The old town also once had 11 towers, 11 gates, 11 bastions, 11 squares, 11 chaplains and 11 guilds. There's even a beer called *Öufi* (local dialect for *elf*, or 11).

The army

Infantry Battalion 11 of the Swiss Army is also known as the Solothurner Battalion. After the reorganisation of the army in 2004, it replaced the old Infantry Regiment 11, which dated back to 1912.

Did you know?
Solothurn, known as Soleure in French, was the home of the French Embassy in Switzerland between 1530 and 1792.

How Food Prices Have Changed

Prices in francs per kilo except eggs and milk (per litre).

	1914	1945	2000
Beef	1.94	4.97	30.94
Bread	0.37	0.54	3.60
Butter	3.89	7.84	16.20
Chocolate	2.10	4.53	16.10
Coffee	2.42	4.70	15.40
One egg	0.12	0.35	0.59
Emmentaler cheese	2.21	4.19	20.10
Flour	0.46	1.58	1.77
Milk	0.23	0.40	1.57
Pasta	0.70	1.20	3.18
Pork	2.33	6.94	20.79
Potatoes	0.13	0.33	1.86
Sugar	0.52	1.21	1.39
Veal	2.36	7.64	59.14
Average monthly income	241	630	5,220

Did you know?
In 1914 the exchange rate between the British pound and Swiss franc was £1 = 25 francs. By 1945 it had dropped to £1 = 17 francs, and in 2000 it was £1 = 2.50 francs. Today it stands at about £1 = 1.45 francs.

The Swiss Abroad

703,640 Swiss citizens live abroad, or about the same as the population of Canton Vaud. Most of them (510,000) have dual nationality and 22% are children.

Europe	435,205		
France	183,754	Africa	20,163
Germany	79,050	South Africa	9,212
Italy	49,555	Americas	174,620
UK	29,778	USA	75,637
Spain	23,978	Canada	39,045
Asia	43,328	Argentina	15,715
Israel	15,172	Oceania	30,326

Where the Swiss Go on Holiday

	Annual numbers
Switzerland	6.6 million
Italy	2.1 million
Germany	1.9 million
France	1.3 million
SE Europe: Greece, Turkey & Balkans	864,000
SW Europe: Spain & Portugal	860,000
Austria	763,000
Rest of Europe	1.0 million
Rest of world	1.3 million

Did you know?

In 2010, the Swiss took a total of 67.9 million day-trips – an average of 10.7 per adult. Those from the German-speaking areas took three times as many day-trips as people in Romandie or Ticino.

Some Treaties with Swiss Names

Treaty of Basel   **22 September 1499**

Peace between the Swiss Confederation and the
Holy Roman Empire, ending the Swabian War
and ensuring Swiss independence

Peace of Basel   **1795**

First   **5 April**

Peace between France and Prussia

Second   **22 July**

Peace between France and Spain

Treaty of Zurich   **10 November 1859**

Peace between France and the Kingdom of
Sardinia on one side and the Austrian Empire
on the other, ending the Austro-Sardinian War

Geneva Convention   **22 August 1864**

Creation of the Red Cross and rules governing
the treatment of wounded soldiers

Treaty of Berne   **9 October 1874**

Creation of the Universal Postal Union

Berne Convention   **9 September 1886**

Protection of Literary and Artistic Works

Treaty of Lausanne   **24 July 1923**

Peace between the Allies (British Empire, France,
Italy, Japan, Greece, Romania & Yugoslavia) and
Turkey. Last peace treaty of World War I

Locarno Pact   16 October 1925

Treaty of Mutual Guarantee (aka the Rhineland
Pact) between Germany, France, Belgium, Great
Britain and Italy

Montreux Convention   20 July 1936

Turkey given full control over the Bosporus and
Dardanelles, plus guarantee of international free
passage through the Straits during peacetime

Zurich Agreement   11 February 1959

New constitution for an independent Cyprus,
plus Treaties of Guarantee and Alliance, signed by
Greece, Turkey, the United Kingdom and Cyprus

Basel Accords   1988

Framework for the standardisation of international
money markets and banks. Basel I (1988) updated
to Basel II (2004) and Basel III (current)

Famous Swiss Brands

Bally	Shoes	1851
Credit Suisse	Banking	1856
Swiss Life	Insurance	1857
Nestlé	Food	1866
UBS	Banking	1872
Schindler	Lifts & escalators	1874
Maggi	Food	1884
Victorinox	Penknives & cutlery	1884
Laufen	Bathrooms	1892
Bernina	Sewing machines	1893
SBB	Railways	1902
Ovomaltine	Drinks	1904
Kuoni	Travel agents	1906
Mont Blanc	Pens	1908
Sigg	Water bottles	1908
Caran d'Ache	Pencils	1924
Thomy	Mustard & mayonnaise	1930
Nescafé	Coffee	1938
Ricola	Herbal drops	1940
Mövenpick	Hotels & restaurants	1948
Zweifel	Potato crisps	1950
Rivella	Soft drinks	1952
Toilet Duck	Bathroom cleaner	1980
Logitech	Computer products	1981
Emmi	Dairy products	1993
Freitag	Bags	1993

Did you know?

The first protected brand name in Switzerland was Swiss Schabziger, a cheese made exclusively in Glarus. The brand and the rules governing it were created on 24 April 1463 by a vote at the Glarus Landsgemeinde, or community parliament.

Sleeping in the Clouds

The Swiss Alpine Club has a network of mountain hikers' huts across the Swiss Alps. In total there are 152 huts, with about 9,300 beds altogether, and all are open the whole year round.

Ten highest Alpine huts

	Height	Beds
Mischabeljochbiwak (VS)	3855m	24
Schalijochbiwak (VS)	3750m	8
Col de la Dent Blanche Bivouac (VS)	3540m	15
Cabane de la Dent Blanche (VS)	3507m	55
Cabane de Bertol (VS)	3311m	80
Berglihütte (BE)	3299m	20
Hornlihütte (VS)	3260m	50
Oberaarjochhütte (VS)	3258m	45
Cabane de Tracuit (VS)	3256m	120
Hollandiahütte (VS)	3238m	70

Did you know?
The largest Alpine hut is the Konkordiahütte (VS) with 150 beds, the smallest are the Refuge de Chalin (VS) and Schalijochbiwak (VS), each with just 8.

Brits in Switzerland

37,273 British citizens live in Switzerland making them the 10th most common nationality, just ahead of Austrians.

Zurich	2,632
Geneva	2,558
Basel	1,496
Lausanne (VD)	747
Nyon (VD)	456
Montreux (VD)	444
Zug	398
Bern	287
Lucerne	275
Chêne-Bougeries (GE)	261
Thalwil (ZH)	255
Küsnacht (ZH)	235
Pully (VD)	233
Baar (ZG)	231
Versoix (GE)	213
Lugano (TI)	209
Winterthur (ZH)	203
Vevey (VD)	202
Reinach (BL)	191
Wädenswil (ZH)	184

Did you know?

Famous British residents currently include Phil Collins, Lewis Hamilton, David Bowie and Roger Moore. Long since departed are the likes of Charlie Chaplin, Richard Burton, Graham Greene, Freddie Mercury, John Knox, and Lord Byron. And of course in 1977-78 a certain Lady Diana Spencer went to the Institut Alpin Videmanette finishing school in Rougemont (VD).

Postcode Regions

Switzerland is divided into nine postcode regions, numbered
from 1 to 9 running west to east across the country, with each
postal location having a four-digit code. The system was
introduced on 26 June 1964, making Switzerland the third
country (after Germany and the USA) to use postcodes.

1000	Lausanne	2000	Neuchâtel
1200	Geneva	2500	Biel/Bienne
1950	Sion	2800	Delémont
3000	Bern	4000	Basel
3600	Thun	4410	Liestal
3900	Brig	4500	Solothurn
5000	Aarau	6000	Lucerne
5200	Brugg	6300	Zug
5400	Baden	6500	Bellinzona
7000	Chur	8000	Zurich
7260	Davos	8400	Winterthur
7500	St Moritz	8750	Glarus
		9000	St Gallen
		9050	Appenzell
		9100	Herisau

Although independent from Switzerland, and with its own
stamps, Liechtenstein is included in the Swiss postal system.
The capital Vaduz has a 9490 postcode.

Did you know?
The General Postal Union was created in Bern on 9 October 1874,
which is now designated World Post Day. It became the Universal
Postal Union in 1878 and has 192 member countries.

Wine Production by Canton

Just over a million hectolitres of Swiss wine are produced every year, almost 90% of it in six cantons. Only 1.7% is exported: it's mainly the Swiss who drink Swiss wine.

	Hectolitres*	% red wine
Valais	397,370	59
Vaud	286,827	28
Geneva	102,968	54
Ticino	53,308	76
Zurich	31,823	65
Neuchâtel	31,618	50
Schaffhausen	30,452	80
Graubünden	24,629	80
Aargau	18,540	68
Thurgau	14,138	66
Bern	13,625	41
Fribourg	8,024	35
St Gallen	7,347	74
Basel-Land	5,513	69
Lucerne	1,922	55
Jura	377	38
Solothurn	337	65
Basel-Stadt	260	47
Appenzell AI & AR	148	55
UR, NW & OW	134	67
Glarus	64	72
Zug	38	35
Switzerland	**1,030,938**	**52**

*1 hectolitre equals 100 litres

Did you know?
70% of the 2.6 million hectolitres of wine consumed every year in Switzerland is red, but only 37% overall is Swiss.

Tunnels and Bridges

There are 793 rail tunnels in Switzerland with a total length of 494.49km.

A chronology of the longest rail tunnels

1858	Hauenstein I	2,495m
1860	Les Loges (Convers)	3,259m
1882	Gotthard I	15,003m
1906	Simplon I	19,803m
1922	Simplon II	19,823m
2004	Lötschberg Base	34,577m
2016	Gotthard NEAT[1]	57,104m

[1]When finished, it will be the longest in the world

A chronology of the longest narrow gauge rail tunnels

1903	Albula	5,865m
1982	Furka Basistunnel	15,442m
1999	Vereina[1]	19,042m

[1]Longest in the world

Longest road tunnels

1980	St Gotthard	16,918m
1980	Seelisberg	9,280m
1967	San Bernardino	6,600m

Did you know?
The 8,250 rail bridges in Switzerland have a total length of 150km. The longest is the Hardturmviadukt (ZH) at 1,134m, the longest single span (150m) belongs to the Lorrainebrücke (BE), and the tallest (99m) is the Sitterviadukt (SG).

Swiss Authors

Some famous Swiss writers and a well-known work (in English, where possible).

Alain de Botton	The Art of Travel
Alex Capus	Sailing by Starlight
Blaise Cendrars	Moravigne
Jacques Chessex	L'Ogre
Selina Chönz	A Bell for Ursli
Friedrich Dürrenmatt	The Visit
Max Frisch	Homo Faber
Friedrich Glauser	In Matto's Realm
Jeremias Gotthelf	The Black Spider
Hermann Hesse	Steppenwolf
Franz Hohler	At Home
Zoe Jenny	The Pollen Room
Gottfried Keller	Green Henry
Pascal Mercier	Night Train to Lisbon
Johanna Spyri	Heidi
Peter Stamm	On a Day like This
Martin Suter	Small World
Erich von Däniken	Chariots of the Gods
Robert Walser	The Assistant
Markus Werner	Zündel's Departure
Johann David Wyss	Swiss Family Robinson

Did you know?

In 2010 there were 10,568 books published in Switzerland and on sale in Swiss bookshops. Of those 5,910 were in German, 2,355 in French, 301 in Italian and 23 in Romansh – and 1,262 in English.

Big Cities and Tiny Villages

There are only 36 communities with a population of more than 20,000, and over half of the Swiss population lives in a community with fewer than 10,000 inhabitants.

Ten largest communities

	Population	Area (km²)
Zurich	372,857	87.9
Geneva	187,470	15.9
Basel	163,216	24.0
Lausanne (VD)	127,821	41.3
Bern	124,381	51.6
Winterthur (ZH)	101,308	68.1
Lucerne	77,491	29.1
St Gallen	72,959	39.3
Lugano (TI)	54,667	32.1
Biel/Bienne (BE)	51,203	21.2

Ten smallest communities

	Population	Area (km²)
Corippo (TI)	12	7.7
Martisberg (VS)	23	3.0
Pigniu (GR)	28	18.0
Mulegns (GR)	30	33.8
Gresso (TI)	31	11.1
Bister (VS)	33	5.8
Cauco (GR)	33	10.9
Selma (GR)	34	2.9
St Martin (GR)	37	22.9
Kammersrohr (SO)	39	0.9

Famous Swiss Americans

The first known Swiss person in what is now the United States was Theobald von Erlach (1541-1565). There are now 75,637 Swiss citizens living in the United States.

Swiss immigrants to the USA

Louis Agassiz	natural scientist
Louis Chevrolet	car maker
Albert Gallatin	politician
Rudolph Ganz	pianist
Meyer Guggenheim	industrialist
Elisabeth Kübler-Ross	psychiatrist
Adolph Rickenbacker	electric guitar maker
Wally Schirra	astronaut
John Sutter	founder of New Helvetia (now Sacramento)
Fritz Zwicky	astronomer

Descended from Swiss immigrants

Steve Ballmer	CEO of Microsoft
Yul Brynner	actor
Warren E Burger	Supreme Court Chief Justice
Peter Buol	first mayor of Las Vegas
Gary Gygax	creator of Dungeons & Dragons
Cyndi Lauper	pop singer
Eddie Rickenbacker	race car driver
Ben Roethlisberger	American footballer
Ryan Seacrest	TV host
Renée Zellweger	actress

Did you know?

Solomon Guggenheim, who founded the iconic art museum in New York that bears his name, was the son of Swiss immigrant Meyer Guggenheim from Aargau. His brother Benjamin was less fortunate; he died on board the Titanic.

Swiss Nobel prize winners

Chemistry

1913	*Alfred Werner
1937	Paul Karrer
1939	*Leopold Ruzicka
1975	*Vladimir Prelog
1991	Richard Robert Ernst
2002	Kurt Wüthrich

Literature

1919	Carl Friedrich Georg Spitteler
1946	*Hermann Hesse

Peace

1901	Henri Dunant
1902	Élie Docommun & Charles Albert Gobat

Physics

1920	Charles-Edouard Guillaume
1921	*Albert Einstein
1952	Felix Bloch
1986	Heinrich Rohrer
1987	Karl Alexander Müller

Physiology or Medicine

1909	Emil Theodor Kocher
1948	Paul Hermann Müller
1949	Walter Rudolf Hess
1950	*Tadeus Reichstein
1951	Max Theiler
1957	Daniel Bovet
1978	Werner Arber
1992	*Edmond Henri Fischer
1996	Rolf Zinkernagel

*Not born in Switzerland but a Swiss citizen at the time of winning

Foreigners in Switzerland

Officially 22.4% of the population are foreigners.

		Overall numbers
Europe		1,504,943 (85% of the total)
	EU-EEA	1,101,501
	Italy	287,130
	Germany	263,271
	Portugal	212,586
	Serbia	121,908
	France	95,643
	Turkey	71,835
	Spain	64,126
	Macedonia	60,116
	Kosovo	58,755
	UK	37,273
Asia		110,549
	Sri Lanka	28,963
	India	10,391
	China	10,268
Africa		71,527
	Eritrea	7,965
	Morocco	7,373
	Tunisia	6,469
North America		25,590
	USA	18,816
	Canada	6,774
Latin America		48,921
	Brazil	17,850
	Dom Republic	5,602
Oceania		3,990
	Australia	3,054
	New Zealand	867
Stateless		230
Total		**1,766,277**

Countries with under 20 residents in Switzerland

Kiribati	1	Papua New Guinea	10
Marshall Islands	1	Surinam	10
Samoa	3	Grenada	11
Solomon Islands	4	Micronesia	11
Vatican City	4	Monaco	11
St Vincent & the Grenadines	5	Vanuatu	12
Tonga	5	Brunei Darussalam	13
East Timor	6	Comoros Islands	13
Western Sahara	7	Equatorial Guinea	14
Polynesia	8	St. Kitts & Nevis	15
Nauru	9	Andorra	16
São Tomé & Principe	9	Belize	17
		Djibouti	19

Did you know?

Of the 1.76 million 'foreigners', 338,740 (or 19%) were born in Switzerland and another 872,000 (or 49%) have been resident longer than five years. In many countries one or other of those reasons would be enough for citizenship. In other words, if Switzerland were to have citizenship and naturalisation rules similar to the USA and Britain, foreigners would constitute only 6.9% of the population.

Women in the Federal Parliament

Swiss women had to wait until 1971 to get the vote or be able to stand for election at a federal level.

First women elected to parliament in 1971

National Council

Elisabeth Blunschy (CVP, SZ)[1]

Tilo Frey (FDP, NE)

Hedi Lang-Gehri (SP, ZH)

Josi Meier, (CVP, LU)[2]

Gabrielle Nanchen, (SP, VS)

Marta Ribi (FDP, ZH)

Liselotte Spreng (FDP, FR)

Hanny Thalmann (CVP, SG)

Lilian Uchtenhagen (SP, ZH)[3]

Nelly Wicky (PdA, GE)

Council of States

Lise Girardin (FDP, GE)

[1]First female National Council president in 1977
[2]First female Council of States president in 1991-2
[3]First female candidate for the Federal Council in 1983

Female members of parliament

In the 11 general elections since 1971, the highest number of women elected was in 2007 with 67, or 27.2% of the 246 seats in both houses of parliament.

	National Council 200 seats	Council of States 46 seats*
1971	10 (5%)	1 (2.2%)
1975	15 (7.5%)	0
1979	21 (10.5%)	3 (6.5%)
1983	22 (11%)	3 (6.5%)
1987	29 (14.5%)	5 (10.9%)
1991	35 (17.5%)	4 (8.7%)
1995	43 (21.5%)	8 (17.4%)
1999	46 (23%)	9 (19.5%)
2003	50 (25%)	11 (23.9%)
2007	57 (28.5%)	10 (21.7%)
2011	57 (28.5%)	9 (19.5%)

*Number of seats increased in 1979 from 44 to 46 when Jura became a canton.

National Hiking Routes

Switzerland has 63,992km of hiking paths, with Graubünden having the most overall (10,608km). Alongside the 60 designated regional and 202 local routes are 7 national ones.

Route 1 **Via Alpina**, 370km, 19 sections: Vaduz - Elm - Altdorf - Meiringen - Lauterbrunnen - Adelboden - Gstaad - Montreux

Route 2 **Trans-Swiss Trail**, 490km, 32 sections: Porrentruy - Neuchâtel - Bern - Sörenberg - Stans - Gotthard - Lugano - Mendrisio

Route 3 **Alpine Panorama Trail**, 510km, 30 sections: Rorschach - Appenzell - Zug - Münsingen - Gruyères - Lausanne - Nyon - Geneva

Route 4 **St Jakobsweg**, 458km, 20 sections: Rorschach - Rapperswil - Schwyz - Brünig - Thun - Fribourg - Lausanne - Geneva

Route 5 **Jura Crest Trail**, 310km, 15 sections: Dielsdorf ZH - Brugg - Hauenstein - Chasseral - Vue des Alpes - Vallorbe - Nyon

Route 6 **Alpine Passes Trail**, 600km, 34 sections: Chur - Ilanz - Airolo - Simplon - Saas Fee - Grand St Bernard - Trient - St Gingolph

Route 7 **Via Gotthardo**, 325km, 20 sections: Basel - Olten - Lucerne - Altdorf - Gotthard - Bellinzona - Lugano - Chiasso

Did you know?
Nationally there are roughly 1.6km of path for every 1km^2 of land; the canton with the densest network of paths is Appenzell Innerrhoden (3.2km per km^2) and the one with the sparsest is Valais (0.6km per km^2).

Births, Deaths, Marriage and Divorce

Births: 80,290
Birth capital of Switzerland: Lausanne (12.6 per 1000 people)
National average: 10.1 per 1000

Lowest cantons: Glarus (8.3) and Graubünden (8.5)
Highest cantons: Vaud (11.6) and Fribourg (11.2)

Deaths: 62,649
Death capital of Switzerland: Basel (11.7 per 1000 people)
National average: 8.1 per 1000

Lowest cantons: Zug (6.0) and Geneva (7.0) and Fribourg (7.0)
Highest cantons: Basel-Stadt (11.5) and Glarus (10.2)

Marriages: 43,257
Marriage capital of Switzerland: Zurich (7.6 per 1000 people)
National average: 5.4 per 1000

Lowest cantons: Uri (4.5) and Glarus (4.6)
Highest cantons: Zurich (6.3) and Zug (5.9) and Appenzell
Innerrhoden (5.9)

Divorces: 22,081
Divorce capital of Switzerland:
La Chaux-de-Fonds (4.2 per 1000 people)
National average: 2.5 per 1000

Lowest cantons: Appenzell Innerrhoden (1.0) and Uri (1.1)
Highest cantons: Neuchâtel (3.6) and Basel-Stadt (3.0)

A Bed for the Night

Switzerland has 245,072 available hotel beds across 128,719 hotel rooms and 4,773 establishments. These are the 20 communities with the most hotel beds:

	Total beds	Establishments
Zurich	12,546	116
Geneva	10,027	87
Zermatt (VS)	6,370	101
Basel	6,273	59
Davos (GR)	5,585	57
Lucerne	5,403	51
St Moritz (GR)	4,454	31
Lausanne (VD)	3,899	34
Bern	3,559	34
Grindelwald (BE)	3,192	48
Interlaken (BE)	3,117	31
Arosa (GR)	2,996	34
Lugano (TI)	2,966	38
Lauterbrunnen[1] (BE)	2,853	44
Opfikon[2] (ZH)	2,447	9
Montreux (VD)	2,399	22
Ascona (TI)	2,290	33
Saas-Fee (VS)	2,166	45
Meyrin[3](GE)	2,069	9
Engelberg (OW)	1,993	27

[1]Includes Wengen & Mürren   [2]Zurich airport   [3]Geneva airport

Did you know?

The largest hotel in Switzerland is the Starling Hotel at Le Grand-Saconnex, beside Geneva airport, with 496 rooms. The highest is the Kulmhotel at Gornergrat, up above Zermatt at 3100m.

Lost Property on Swiss Trains

Ten most commonly found articles

1	Coats & jackets	10,746
2	Mobile phones	10,289
3	Shopping bags	9,733
4	Rucksacks	9,152
5	Wallets & purses	6,401
6	Holdalls & sports bags	6,246
7	Keys	5,878
8	Spectacles	3,739
9	Hats & headgear	3,477
10	Gloves	2,625

Did you know?

Of the 105,000 articles left behind on SBB trains in 2010, some were rather unusual: a glass eye, a pizza oven (40kg), false teeth, a wedding dress, a heart catheter, a poison ring (without the poison), a parachute, a plastic skull, and all the necessaries for a Mass – chalice, bible, consecrated wafers, & wine. Oddest of all, perhaps, were Grandma's gallstones (from 1966).

Potatoes – a National Vegetable

The Swiss love their potatoes, eating an average of 46.3kg per person per year, with the most popular ways being mashed, Rösti and chips. Over 11,000 hectares of land is used to grow potatoes, half of it in Cantons Bern and Vaud.

The main varieties are divided into three colour-coded groups for selling:

Type A coded green
Waxy and suitable for potato salad, raclette and boiled potatoes: Annabelle, Charlotte, Ditta, Nicola

Type B coded red
Mainly waxy and suitable for Rösti, roast potatoes and chips: Agata, Jelly, Lady Christi, Lady Felicia, Laura, Victoria

Type C coded blue
Floury and suitable for mashed potato, baked potatoes, gnocchi, and gratin: Agria, Bintje, Derby, Désirée

The American Food Invasion

McDonald's
First Swiss branch: 1976 in Geneva
Branches now: 151
Employees: 7,300

Burger King
First Swiss branch: 1981 in Lugano
Branches now: 30
Employees: 900

Starbucks
First Swiss branch: 2001 in Zurich
Branches now: 49
Employees: 670

Lake Paddle Steamers

All these elegant boats are still in operation.

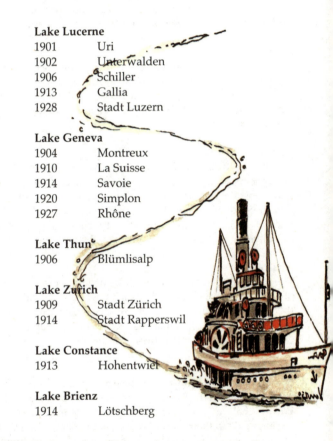

Lake Lucerne

1901	Uri
1902	Unterwalden
1906	Schiller
1913	Gallia
1928	Stadt Luzern

Lake Geneva

1904	Montreux
1910	La Suisse
1914	Savoie
1920	Simplon
1927	Rhône

Lake Thun

1906	Blümlisalp

Lake Zürich

1909	Stadt Zürich
1914	Stadt Rapperswil

Lake Constance

1913	Hohentwiel

Lake Brienz

1914	Lötschberg

The journey from Lucerne to Flüelen covers 38.1km and takes 2 hours and 43 minutes by paddlesteamer. It forms part of the William Tell Express scenic train and boat ride linking Lucerne and Lugano or Locarno.

The Original Geneva Convention

Article 1.
Ambulances and military hospitals shall be recognized as neutral, and as such, protected and respected by the belligerents as long as they accommodate wounded and sick. Neutrality shall end if the said ambulances or hospitals should be held by a military force.

Article 2.
Hospital and ambulance personnel, including the quarter-master's staff, the medical, administrative and transport services, and the chaplains, shall have the benefit of the same neutrality when on duty, and while there remain any wounded to be brought in or assisted.

Article 3.
The persons designated in the preceding Article may, even after enemy occupation, continue to discharge their functions in the hospital or ambulance with which they serve, or may withdraw to rejoin the units to which they belong. When in these circumstances they cease from their functions, such persons shall be delivered to the enemy outposts by the occupying forces.

Article 4.
The material of military hospitals being subject to the laws of war, the persons attached to such hospitals may take with them, on withdrawing, only the articles which are their own personal property. Ambulances, on the contrary, under similar circumstances, shall retain their equipment.

Article 5.
Inhabitants of the country who bring help to the wounded shall be respected and shall remain free. Generals of the belligerent Powers shall make it their duty to notify the inhabitants of the appeal made to their humanity, and of the neutrality which humane conduct will confer. The presence of any wounded combatant receiving shelter and care in a house shall ensure its protection. An inhabitant who has given shelter to the wounded shall be exempted from billeting and from a portion of such war contributions as may be levied.

Article 6.
Wounded or sick combatants, to whatever nation they may belong, shall be collected and cared for. Commanders-in-Chief may hand over immediately to the enemy outposts enemy combatants wounded during an engagement, when circumstances allow and subject to the agreement of both parties. Those who, after their recovery, are recognized as being unfit for further service, shall be repatriated. The others may likewise be sent back, on condition that they shall not again, for the duration of hostilities, take up arms. Evacuation parties, and the personnel conducting them, shall be considered as being absolutely neutral.

Article 7.
A distinctive and uniform flag shall be adopted for hospitals, ambulances and evacuation parties. It should in all circumstances be accompanied by the national flag. An armlet may also be worn by personnel enjoying neutrality but its issue shall be left to the military authorities. Both flag and armlet shall bear a red cross on a white ground.

Article 8.
The implementing of the present Convention shall be arranged by the Commanders-in-Chief of the belligerent armies following the instructions of their respective Governments and in accordance with the general principles set forth in this Convention.

Article 9.
The High Contracting Parties have agreed to communicate the present Convention with an invitation to accede thereto to Governments unable to appoint Plenipotentiaries to the International Conference at Geneva. The Protocol has accordingly been left open.

Article 10.
The present Convention shall be ratified and the ratifications exchanged at Berne, within the next four months, or sooner if possible.

Did you know?
The original signatories of the first Geneva Convention on 22 August 1864, were Baden, Belgium, Denmark, France, Hesse, Holland, Italy, Portugal, Prussia, Spain, Switzerland, and Wurtemberg.

Who Has the Most Cows?

There are almost 1.6 million cows in Switzerland, or about one for every five people. In Appenzell Innerrhoden, the ratio is almost 1:1, whereas in Geneva there are 174 people for every cow. The ratio given below is cows:people.

	Cows	Ratio		Cows	Ratio
Bern	320,581	1:3	Valais	31,878	1:10
Lucerne	151,076	1:2	Basel-Land & Basel-Stadt	28,847	1:16
St Gallen	141,464	1:3	Appenzell AR	23,327	1:2
Fribourg	135,227	1:2	Zug	20,197	1:6
Vaud	115,066	1:6	Obwalden	18,070	1:2
Zurich	95,020	1:14	Schaffhausen	16,353	1:5
Aargau	88,543	1:7	Appenzell AI	14,956	1:1
Graubünden	75,525	1:3	Nidwalden	12,472	1:3
Thurgau	74,532	1:3	Uri	12,111	1:3
Jura	59,591	1:1	Glarus	11,797	1:3
Solothurn	44,982	1:6	Ticino	10,485	1:32
Schwyz	44,669	1:3	Geneva	2,621	1:175
Neuchâtel	41,843	1:4			
Switzerland	**1,591,233**	**1:5**			

Did you know?
The most crowded (or maybe cow-ded) canton is Lucerne, with 101.2 cows per km^2, well above the national average of 38. The least crowded cow-wise is Ticino, with a mere 3.7 per km^2; even Geneva manages 9.3.

Highest Point of each Canton

		metres
Valais	Dufourspitze*	4634
Bern	Finsteraarhorn	4274
Graubünden	Piz Bernina	4049
Uri	Dammastock	3630
Glarus	Tödi: Piz Russein	3614
Ticino	Rheinwaldhorn / Adula	3402
St Gallen	Ringelspitz	3248
Obwalden	Titlis	3238
Vaud	Les Diablerets	3210
Nidwalden	Rotstöckli	2901
Schwyz	Bös Fulen	2802
Appenzell AI	Säntis	2502
Appenzell AR	Säntis	2502
Fribourg	Vanil Noir	2389
Lucerne	Brienzer Rothorn	2350
Zug	Wildspitz	1580
Neuchâtel	Chasseral	1552
Solothurn	Hasenmatt	1445
Jura	Mont Raimeux	1302
Zurich	Schnebelhorn	1292
Basel-Land	Hinteri Egg	1169
Thurgau	Hohgrat	991
Schaffhausen	Hagen	912
Aargau	Geissfluegrat	908
Basel-Stadt	St Chrischona	522
Geneva	Les Arales	516

*Also known as Monte Rosa

Switzerland in 1850

The first complete national population census took place in 1850. Here is how Switzerland looked then.

Switzerland	2,392,740
German-speaking	70.2%
French-speaking	22.6%
Italian-speaking	5.4%
Romansh-speaking	1.8%
Catholic	40.6%
Protestant	59.2%
Foreigners	3%

Cantonal populations[1]

Bern[2]	458,301	Geneva	64,146
Zurich	250,698	Basel-Land	47,885
Aargau	199,852	Schwyz	44,168
Vaud	199,575	Appenzell AR	43,621
St Gallen	169,625	Schaffhausen	35,300
Lucerne	132,843	Glarus	30,213
Ticino	117,759	Basel-Stadt	29,698
Fribourg	99,891	Zug	17,461
Graubünden	89,895	Uri	14,505
Thurgau	88,908	Obwalden	13,799
Valais	81,559	Nidwalden	11,339
Neuchâtel	70,753	Appenzell AI	11,272
Solothurn	69,674		

[1]For current cantonal populations, see page 52.
[2]including what is now Canton Jura, population then 31,542

20 largest towns in 1850

Two main centres of watch-making – La Chaux-de-Fonds and
Le Locle – were big places in the 19th century, relatively speaking.
Their population increase since then has been noticeably less than
in other towns.

	1850	Now	Increase
Geneva	31,238	187,470	500%
Bern	27,558	124,381	351%
Basel	27,313	163,216	498%
Lausanne (VD)	17,108	127,821	647%
Zurich	17,040	372,857	2088%
La Chaux-de-Fonds (NE)	12,638	37,504	197%
St Gallen	11,234	72,959	549%
Lucerne	10,068	77,491	670%
Fribourg	9,065	34,897	285%
Le Locle (NE)	8,514	10,049	18%
Herisau (AR)	8,387	15,236	82%
Neuchâtel	7,727	33,054	328%
Schaffhausen	7,700	34,943	354%
Altstätten (SG)	6,492	10,819	67%
Chur (GR)	6,183	33,756	446%
Köniz (BE)	5,984	38,823	549%
Schwyz	5,432	14,423	166%
Solothurn	5,370	16,066	199%
Winterthur (ZH)	5,341	101,308	1797%
Vevey (VD)	5,201	18,394	254%

In the same period the population of Switzerland increased by
229%.

The Swiss Army Knife

In 1891 the Swiss Army was first supplied with soldiers' knives by Victorinox, as the company is now known. The Swiss Officer's Knife followed in 1897.

Spartan (standard officer's knife)
Length 91mm, width 26.5mm, height 15mm, weight 60g

12 tools:

large blade	key ring
small blade	toothpick
can opener with	tweezers
small screwdriver	cap lifter with
corkscrew	screwdriver
reamer	wire stripper

Other standard models (with number of tools)

Camper	13	Mountaineer	18
Climber	14	Ranger	21
Huntsman	15	Handyman	24
Explorer	16	Traveller	25
Angler	18		

Swiss Champ (largest standard officer's knife)

Length 91mm, width 27mm, height 33mm, weight 187g

33 tools:
- large blade
- small blade
- can opener with
    - small screwdriver
- corkscrew
- reamer
- wood saw
- screwdriver 2.5mm
- Philips screwdriver
- chisel
- key ring
- toothpick
- tweezers
- mini-screwdriver
- steel pin
- multi-purpose hook
- sewing eye
- pliers with
    - wire crimping tool
    - wire cutters
- cap lifter with
    - screwdriver
    - wire stripper
- scissors
- ballpoint pen
- fish scaler with
    - hook disgorger
    - ruler (cm + inches)
- magnifying lens (5x)
- nail file with
    - metal file
    - nail cleaner
    - metal saw

Swiss soldier's knife (Swiss army issue knife)

Length 111mm, width 34.5mm, height 18mm, weight 131g

Tools:
- can opener with
    - small screwdriver
- corkscrew
- reamer
- wood saw
- Philips screwdriver
- key ring
- strong screwdriver with
    - cap lifter
    - wire stripper
- lock blade for one-hand opening

Did you know?

The company name Victorinox was created in 1921. It comes from the contraction of two words: Victoria, the mother of company founder Karl Elsener, and inox, another word for stainless steel.

Famous Foreign Graves

Canton Geneva
- Jorge Luis Borges, Argentinian author: (†1986) Plainpalais Cemetery Geneva
- Richard Burton, British actor: (†1984) Celigny
- Jean Calvin, French reformer: (†1564) Plainpalais Cemetery Geneva
- Sir Humphrey Davy, British scientist: (†1829) Plainpalais Cemetery Geneva
- Alistair MacLean, British author: (†1987) Celigny

Canton Vaud
- Coco Chanel, French designer: (†1971) Bois-de-Vaux Cemetery, Lausanne
- Charlie Chaplin, British actor: (†1977) Corsier-sur-Vevey
- Pierre de Coubertin, French Olympic founder: (†1937) Bois-de-Vaux Cemetery, Lausanne
- Graham Greene, British author: (†1991) Corsier-sur-Vevey
- Audrey Hepburn, Belgian actress: (†1993) Tolochenaz
- James Mason, British actor: (†1984) Corsier-sur-Vevey
- Vladimir Nabokov, Russian author: (†1977) Clarens
- Henri Nestlé, German industrialist: (†1890) Territet
- David Niven, British actor: (†1983) Chateau d'Oex
- Peter Ustinov, British actor: (†2004) Nyon

Ticino
- Paulette Goddard, American actress: (†1990) Ronco sopra Ascona
- Hermann Hesse, German author: (†1962) Montagnola
- Patricia Highsmith, American author: (†1995) Tegna
- Robert Palmer, British singer: (†2003) Lugano
- Erich Maria Remarque, German author: (†1970) Ronco sopra Ascona

German-speaking Switzerland
- Elias Canetti, German author: (†1994) Fluntern Cemetery, Zurich
- Erasmus, Dutch thinker: (†1536) Basel Cathedral
- James Joyce, Irish author: (†1941) Fluntern Cemetery, Zurich
- Paul Klee, German artist: (†1940) Schosshalde Cemetery, Bern
- Thomas Mann, German author: (†1955) Kilchberg (ZH)
- Meret Oppenheim, German artist: (†1985) Birsfelden Cemetery, Basel
- Elisabeth Schwarzkopf, German singer: (†2006) Zumikon Cemetery, Zurich

Did you know?

Two European queens died in Switzerland, though both were buried in their homelands.

Queen Astrid of Belgium (and princess of Sweden) died on 29 August 1935 in a car crash aged 29. A chapel near Küssnacht am Rigi (LU) commemorates the tragedy.

Elisabeth, Empress of Austria and Queen of Hungary, was assassinated in Geneva by Luigi Lucheni, an Italian anarchist. Sissi, as she was popularly known, died on 10 September 1898 aged 61. Her statue stands on Geneva's lakefront.

Across the Röstigraben

French is the second language of Switzerland, with the majority of its 1.6 million speakers found in the western part of the country: La Romandie. The imaginary divide between Romandie and the rest of Switzerland is known as the Röstigraben* – but what if that was a real border?

Romandie as an independent nation would consist of the cantons of Geneva, Vaud, Neuchâtel and Jura plus most of Canton Fribourg, half of Valais and the northwestern chunk of Canton Bern. Its area would be roughly 8,650km², or about the same as Puerto Rico, with a population similar in size to Qatar.

Largest towns in Romandie:

	Population		Population
Geneva	187,470	Vernier (GE)	32,844
Lausanne	127,821	Sion (VS)	30,363
La Chaux-de-Fonds (NE)	37,504	Lancy (GE)	28,631
Fribourg	34,897	Yverdon-les-Bains (VD)	27,511
Neuchâtel	33,054	Montreux (VD)	24,579

Biel/Bienne (BE) is officially bilingual and with 51,203 inhabitants could be classed as the third largest town if it were to be included as part of Romandie. However, the percentage of French speakers is 28.1%, or only 14,388 people.

Did you know?

Zurich would be the 30th largest town in Romandie, based on the number of French-speaking inhabitants. Its French-speaking population is about the same size as Gland or Moutier

*The term refers to *Rösti*, a dish of fried grated potatoes that is typical for the German-speaking part of Switzerland, and *Graben*, a ditch.

Swiss Coins

There are seven Swiss coins in circulation

5 franc

Weight	13.2g	Thickness	2.35mm
Diameter	31.45mm	Last redesign	1931

Inscription on edge: DOMINUS PROVIDEBIT and 13 stars

2 franc

Weight	8.80g	Thickness	2.15mm
Diameter	27.4mm	Last redesign	1874

1 franc

Weight	4.40g	Thickness	1.55mm
Diameter	23.2mm	Last redesign	1875

½ franc

Weight	2.20g	Thickness	1.25mm
Diameter	18.2mm	Last redesign	1875

20 rappen

Weight	4.0g	Thickness	1.65mm
Diameter	21.05mm	Last redesign	1881

10 rappen

Weight	3.0g	Thickness	1.45mm
Diameter	19.15mm	Last redesign	1879

5 rappen

Weight	1.80g	Thickness	1.25mm
Diameter	17.15mm	Last redesign	1879

Although the designs have not changed, the metals have. Until 1967, the franc coins (½, 1, 2 and 5) were made from silver. Since 1969 all have been produced in cupronickel (75% copper, 25% nickel), the same as the 20 and 10 rappen. The 5 rappen piece has been 92% copper, 6% aluminium, 2% nickel since 1981.

Did you know?

Switzerland has the highest per capita gold reserves in the world, followed by Lebanon and Germany.

The Swiss Path

The Swiss Path alongside Lake Uri was inaugurated in 1991, with
the length of path for each canton determined by the size of its
population at that time. The cantons are placed along the path in
the order they joined the confederation.

1291	Uri	182m	1501	Schaffhausen	376m
1291	Schwyz	544m	1513	Appenzell AR	263m
1291	Obwalden	146m	1513	Appenzell AI	71m
1291	Nidwalden	163m	1803	St Gallen	2,152m
1332	Lucerne	1,632m	1803	Graubünden	890m
1351	Zurich	6,089m	1803	Aargau	2,506m
1352	Glarus	197m	1803	Thurgau	1,019m
1352	Zug	424m	1803	Ticino	1,475m
1353	Bern	4,980m	1803	Vaud	2,907m
1481	Fribourg	1,026m	1815	Valais	1,227m
1481	Solothurn	1,179m	1815	Neuchâtel	836m
1501	Basel-Stadt	1,072m	1815	Geneva	1,951m
1501	Basel-Land	1,206m	1979	Jura	348m

EU-Swiss Bilateral Agreements

Bilaterals I
Signed 1999, approved by referendum 2000
Free movement of persons
Technical barriers to trade
Public procurement markets
Agriculture
Research
Civil aviation
Overland transport

Bilaterals II
Signed 2004, approved by parliament 2004
Schengen/Dublin (approved by referendum 2005)
Taxation of savings
Processed agricultural products
MEDIA film programme
Environment
Statistics
Fight against fraud
Pensions
Education & vocational training
(signed 2010, approved by parliament 2010)

Federal Elections since 1971

1971 was the first year with universal adult suffrage in Switzerland; until then women could not vote in federal elections.

National Council
200 seats divided up by canton and population.

Year Turnout	Seats Vote %					
	FDP	**CVP**	**SP**	**SVP**	**Greens**	**Others**
2011	30	28	46	54	15	27
48.5%	15.1%	12.3%	18.7%	26.6%	8.4%	18.9%
2007	31*	31	43	62	20	13
48.3%	15.8%	14.5%	19.5%	28.9%	9.6%	11.7%
2003	36	28	52	55	13	16
45.2%	17.3%	14.4%	23.3%	26.7%	7.4%	10.9%
1999	43	35	51	44	9	18
43.3%	19.9%	15.9%	22.5%	22.5%	5.0%	14.2%
1995	45	34	54	29	8	30
42.2%	20.2%	16.8%	21.8%	14.9%	5.0%	21.3%
1991	44	35	41	25	14	41
46.0%	21.0%	18.0%	18.5%	11.9%	6.1%	24.5%
1987	51	42	41	25	9	32
46.5%	22.9%	19.6%	18.4%	11.0%	4.9%	23.2%
1983	54	42	47	23	3	31
48.9%	23.3%	20.6%	22.8%	11.1%	1.9%	20.3%
1979	51	44	51	23	1	30
48%	24.0%	21.3%	24.4%	11.6%	0.6%	18.1%
1975	47	46	55	21	0	31
52.4%	22.2%	21.1%	24.9%	9.9%	0.1%	21.8%
1971	49	44	46	23	-	38
56.9%	21.8%	20.3%	22.9%	11.1%		23.9%

*FDP & Liberals merged in 2009. Combined totals in 2007 = 35 seats, 17.7%

First National Council president:
Ulrich Ochsenbein (FDP, BE) 1848

First female National Council president:
Elisabeth Blunschy (CVP, SZ) 1977

Council of States

46 seats divided up by canton

	FDP	CVP	SP	SVP	Others
2011	11	13	11	5	6
2007	12	15	9	7	3
2003	14	15	9	8	0
1999	17	15	6	7	1
1995	17	16	5	5	3
1991	18	16	3	4	5
1987	14	19	5	4	4
1983	14	18	6	5	3
1979*	11	18	9	5	3
1975	15	17	5	5	2
1971	15	17	4	5	3

*Numbers of seats increased from 44 to 46 when Jura became a canton

First Council of States president: Jonas Furrer (FDP, ZH) 1848

First female Council of States president: Josi Meier, (CVP, LU) 1991

The Swiss Flag

The square red flag with a white cross in the middle is an iconic symbol of Switzerland. Since 1 January 2007 its red has been defined as Pantone 485 – an equal mixture of magenta and yellow.

Although the square shape of the flag is not set by law, the shape of the central cross is. On 12 December 1889 the government prescribed that each of the four arms be of equal length but one-sixth longer than it is broad.

Did you know?
There are six animals shown on the cantonal flags – bear (AI, AR, BE), bull (UR), eagle (GE), ibex (GR), lion (TG), ram (SH) – plus a man (GL).

Number of National Council Seats by Canton

	Seats	Inhabitants per seat
Appenzell Ausserrhoden	1	53,017
Valais	7	44,669
Ticino	8	41,719
Geneva	11	41,610
Thurgau	6	41,407
Nidwalden	1	41,024
Aargau	15	40,764
Zurich	34	40,384
St Gallen	12	39,909
Fribourg	7	39,785
Vaud	18	39,627
Switzerland	**200**	**39,350**
Basel-Land	7	39,201
Glarus	1	38,608
Graubünden	5	38,524
Schaffhausen	2	38,178
Lucerne	10	37,761
Zug	3	37,702
Bern	26	37,685
Basel-Stadt	5	36,990
Schwyz	4	36,683
Solothurn	7	36,469
Obwalden	1	35,585
Uri	1	35,422
Jura	2	35,016
Neuchâtel	5	34,417
Appenzell Innerrhoden	1	15,688

As small half-cantons the two Appenzells have the minimum one seat each, making them appear very over- and under-represented. Together they would have an average of 34,352 inhabitants per seat.

The U17 Worldbeaters

On 15 November 2009, the Swiss football team won the Under-17 World Cup, beating hosts Nigeria in the final. The only goal was scored by Haris Seferovic, one of 13 Swiss players who either were originally born abroad or were 'Secondos' (second-generation born in Switzerland).

Nassim Ben Khalifa	Tunisia
André Gonçalves	Portugal
Sead Hajrovic	Bosnia-Hercegovina
Pajtim Kasani	Albania
Joel Kiassumbua	Congo
Igor Mijatovic	Serbia
Maik Nakic	Croatia
Kofi Nimeley	Ghana
Ricardo Rodriguez	Chile
Haris Seferovic	Bosnia-Hercegovina
Robin Vecchi	Italy
Frédéric Veseli	Kosovo
Granit Xhaka	Albania

Oldest Football Clubs

Twelve clubs still playing in the current leagues were founded before 1900

1879	FC St Gallen	1896	Lausanne-Sports
1886	Grasshopper Club Zurich	1896	FC Winterthur
1890	Servette FC	1896	FC Zurich
1893	FC Basel	1898	BSC Young Boys
1894	FC La Chaux-de-Fonds	1898	FC Etoile-Sporting
1896	FC Biel/Bienne	1898	FC Thun

Most Visited Tourist Attractions

The Matterhorn and Lucerne's Chapel Bridge may be the most photographed places in Switzerland, but here are the attractions that have the most paid entries:

	Visitors
Zurich Zoo	1.8 million
Basel Zoo	1.7 million
Rhine Falls (SH)	1.1 million
Swiss Transport Museum, Lucerne	927,000
Nature and Animal Park, Goldau (SZ)	885,000
Kunstmuseum Basel	665,000
Emmentaler Cheesery, Affoltern (BE)	332,000
Swiss Aqua Parc, Bouveret (VS)	315,000
Chateau de Chillon (VD)	313,000
Ballenberg Open Air Museum (BE)	310,000

Down the Rhine

The Rhine is Switzerland's longest river, running for 375km through the country and along its borders with Liechtenstein, Austria and Germany.

Lake Toma (source of the Rhine) – Sedrun – Disentis/Mustér – Trun – Ilanz – Reichenau (Voderrhein and Hinterrhein meet) – Domat/Ems – Felsberg – Chur – Landquart – Bad Ragaz – Buchs SG – Diepoldsau – St. Margrethen – Rheineck – Lake Constance – Kreuzlingen – Untersee – Stein am Rhein – Diessenhofen – Büsingen am Hochrhein (German enclave) – Schaffhausen – Rhine Falls – Rheinau – Eglisau – Kaiserstuhl – Rümikon – Bad Zurzach – Koblenz (Rhine and Aare meet) – Etzgen – Laufenburg – Stein AG – Wallbach – Rheinfelden – Kaiseraugst – Birsfelden – Basel – Swiss border

Did you know?
The Rhine Falls are Europe's largest waterfalls: 150m wide, 23m high and with 700,000 litres per second going over when water levels are at their peak.

The Top of Europe

Europe's highest train station sits at Jungfraujoch, 3454 metres above sea level. It opened on 1 August 1912 after 16 years of construction from the route's start at Kleine Scheidegg station.

First plans drawn up	27 August 1893
Federal Council grants the concession	21 December 1894
Construction begins at Kleine Scheidegg	27 July 1896
Eigergletscher station opens	19 September 1898
Eigerwand station opens	28 June 1903
Eismeer station opens	25 July 1905
Final breakthrough at Jungfraujoch	21 February 1912
Total distance	9.34km
Height difference	1393m
Gauge	1000mm
Budget	CHF 7.4 million
Final cost	CHF 16 million
Daily wage for a tunneller in 1897	4.60 francs
Number of deaths during construction	30
Number of strikes during construction	6
Annual passenger numbers:	
1913	42,880
2011	765,000

Did you know?
The line's Swiss architect, Adolf Guyer-Zeller, originally planned for it to go up to the summit of the Jungfrau. That never happened and he never saw much of the line completed; he died on 3 April 1899.

The United States of Switzerland

New Glarus, Wisconsin, isn't quite as well known as some other 'New' places in America but it is home to the Swiss Center of North America. Founded in 1845 by 108 settlers from old Glarus, it now has 2,073 inhabitants (35% of them with Swiss ancestry). And it's not the only Swiss placename in America – according to the US Geological Survey, there are also:

Switzerland
There's a Switzerland County in Indiana plus two lakes, two populated places* and various Little Switzerlands dotted around the country

Geneva
The most numerous, with a Geneva County in Alabama, 35 populated places* called Geneva, 27 Lake Genevas (all of which are lakes or reservoirs – except two that are towns), and five streams, three summits, a canal, an island and a bay

Lucerne
Lucerne manages 17 populated places*, 14 lakes (two of which are towns), three valleys and a mountain. Luzerne (sic) has a county in Pennsylvania, plus seven towns and a lake

Bern
Four populated places* plus a peak and a lake, as well as Berne (12 populated places*), Newbern, Bernville and Bernstadt

Interlaken
Five populated places* plus one Interlachen

Zurich
Four populated places* and one Lake Zurich

Matterhorn
Nine mountains plus, rather oddly, a Matterhorn Canyon in California

Not forgetting Montreux in Florida, Neuchatel in Kansas, Schweizer in Kentucky, Winterthur in Delaware and Vevay (sic) in Switzerland County, Indiana.

Did you know?
New Bern, North Carolina, was founded in 1710 by Christoph von Graffenried, from Bern. He was given the land by Queen Anne and arrived with 150 settlers. The city was the state's first capital and became the birthplace of Pepsi-Cola, invented in 1898 by local pharmacist Caleb Bradham.

* "Place or area with clustered or scattered buildings and a permanent human population (city, settlement, town, village)"

Counting the Animals

Aargau is the rabbit capital of Switzerland and Canton Lucerne has the most pigs, but Canton Bern is definitely the biggest farm in Switzerland. For every category of livestock, Bern is one of the top two cantons, giving it a total of 2.2 million farm animals, or more than two for every person.

Livestock populations in Switzerland

Chickens		8,943,676
	Fribourg	1,537,603
	Bern	1,448,459
Cows		1,591,233
	Bern	320,581
	Lucerne	151,076
Pigs		1,588,998
	Lucerne	423,185
	Bern	281,005
Sheep		434,083
	Valais	62,756
	Bern	60,552
Rabbits		100,107
	Aargau	26,465
	Bern	24,896
Goats		86,987
	Bern	15,352
	Ticino	11,984
Horses		62,113
	Bern	11,058
	Vaud	5,779

Bernese Men

In Bern most men's names are given a shortened form ending in 'u'. Here are some of my favourites.

Adrian	Ädu
Alexander	Xändu
Andreas	Ändu
Beat	Bidu
Christian	Chrigu
Daniel	Dänu
Felix	Fixu
Hanspeter	Hämpu or Schämpu
Hermann	Mändu
Joel	Schölu
Jonathan	Jönu
Klaus	Chlöisu
Markus	Küsu
Martin	Tinu
Michel	Mischu
Pascal	Päscu
Patrick	Pädu
Philip	Fippu
Robert	Röbu
Samuel	Sämu

Imports and Exports

In 2011 the Swiss balance of trade saw a record surplus of 23.8 billion francs. The main imports are consumer goods, raw materials, pharmaceuticals, machinery and energy; the main exports, pharmaceuticals, chemicals, watches, foodstuffs and machinery.

Main import partners

Germany	33.6%	USA	4.5%
Italy	10.9%	China	3.6%
France	8.9%	Ireland	3.4%
Netherlands	4.6%	UK	3.3%
Austria	4.5%	Belgium	2.8%

Total annual imports
CHF 173.7 billion 79% from EU countries

Main export partners

Germany	20.2%	UK	4.2%
USA	10.1%	Japan	3.2%
Italy	7.9%	Hong Kong	3.2%
France	7.9%	Austria	3%
China	4.3%	Spain	2.9%

Total annual exports
CHF 197.6 billion 62% to EU countries

Package Pioneers

Thomas Cook's first package tour to Switzerland took place in the summer of 1863: a 21-day tour from London to Lucerne and back with the following itinerary.

Travel London to Paris via Newhaven and Dieppe
Paris – Geneva – Chamonix – Mer de Glace – Martigny – Sion – Leukerbad – Gemmi Pass – Kandersteg – Spiez – Interlaken – Lauterbrunnen – Wengen – Grindelwald – Giessbach – Brienz – Lucerne – Weggis – Rigi – Lucerne – Olten – Neuchâtel – Paris
Travel back to London via Dieppe and Newhaven

Foreign Visitors

Over 8.5 million foreign tourists arrived in Switzerland in 2011, just outnumbering the 7.7 million 'arrivals' from Swiss tourists travelling within the country.

	Annual numbers		Annual numbers
Germany	2 million	India	201,000
United Kingdom	682,000	Russia	179,000
France	681,000	Austria	190,000
United States	669,000	South Korea	115,000
Italy	48,000	Australia	106,000
China	453,000	Canada	99,000
The Netherlands	338,000	Sweden	86,000
Japan	276,000	Brazil	79,000
Spain	229,000	Israel	65,000
Belgium	215,000	Denmark	57,000

Biggest Swiss Employers

There are 4.7 million people employed in Switzerland, roughly 60% of the population. Unemployment in 2011 stood at 191,000, or 4.2%.

Company	Employees in Switzerland
Migros Group	83,616
Coop Group	53,559
Die Post	37,863
Federal Government	36,859
SBB	28,142
Swatch Group	25,197
UBS	23,284
Credit Suisse	21,700
Swisscom	20,032
Novartis	12,500

Switzerland in Different Languages

In its own four languages Switzerland is known as Schweiz, Suisse, Svizzera and Svizra. The rest of the world has its own versions:

Afrikaans	Switserland	Japanese	スイス
Albanian	Zvicer	Korean	스위스
Arabic	سويسرا	Latvian	Šveice
Basque	Suitza	Lithuanian	Šveicarija
Catalan	Suïssa	Maltese	Żvizzera
Chinese	瑞 士	Norwegian	Sveits
Croatian	Švicarska	Polish	Szwajcaria
Czech	Švýcarsko	Portuguese	Suíça
Danish	Schweiz	Romanian	Elveția
Dutch	Zwitserland	Russian	Швейцария
Esperanto	Svislando	Serbian	Švajcarska
Estonian	Šveits	Slovenian	Švica
Finnish	Sveitsi	Spanish	Suiza
Greek	Ελβετία	Swahili	Uswisi
Hebrew	שווייץ	Swedish	Schweiz
Hindi	स्विट्जरलैंड	Tagalog	Suwisa
Hungarian	Svájc	Tamil	ஸ்விஸ்
Icelandic	Sviss	Turkish	İsviçre
Irish	An Eilvéis	Vietnamese	Thụy Sĩ
		Welsh	Swistir

Did you know?

The official name for Switzerland is Confœderatio Helvetica, the Latin version of Swiss Confederation; it is shortened to CH for the international country code.

Cheese Production

The Swiss produced 181,675 tonnes of cheese in 2011, of which 35% was exported, primarily to Germany and Italy. Just less than 49,000 tonnes of cheese were imported, mainly from Italy, France and Germany. British cheese accounted for only 0.3% of imports.

Popular types	Tonnes produced
Le Gruyère AOC	28,691
Emmentaler AOC	25,256
Mozzarella	20,558
Swiss Raclette	10,786
Appenzeller	9,096
Tilsiter	3,603
Vacherin Fribourgeois AOC	2,574
Walliser Raclette AOC	2,132
Tête de Moine AOC	2,075
Sbrinz AOC	1,939

Did you know?
Emmentaler AOC is the most exported Swiss cheese, with over 17,400 tonnes, or 70% of the annual production, sent abroad, half of it going to Italy alone. Le Gruyère AOC is a distant second, with 11,700 tonnes (or 41% of production) exported, and Germany as the biggest customer.

The Swiss Arms Trade

Switzerland exported military material to 68 different countries in 2011, earning over CHF 873 million and making it a record year. The top two importers accounted for half of all the sales.

Top 20 importers of Swiss weapons

United Arab Emirates (UAE)	Denmark
Germany	France
Italy	Brazil
Belgium	Singapore
Spain	Sweden
USA	India
Norway	Greece
United Kingdom	Pakistan
Netherlands	Australia
Saudi Arabia	South Africa

Military exports by type

33.1%	Aircraft
21.4%	Tanks and other vehicles
18.6%	Ammunition for guns
12.3%	Firing guidance systems
8.9%	Guns other than handguns
2.7%	Military fuel
2.5%	Handguns
0.4%	Bombs, torpedoes and rockets

Did you know?
The UAE bought 25 training jets, which normally don't count as military exports; aircraft typically make up only 4% of the Swiss arms trade. However the government could not guarantee the planes would not be fitted with missiles at some point. Such is the fine line between trade and war.

Main Swiss Motorways

A1	French border – Geneva – Lausanne – Bern – Zurich – St Margrethen
A2	German border – Basel – Lucerne – Gotthard Tunnel – Lugano – Chiasso
A3	French border – Basel – Baden – Zurich – Sargans
A4	German border – Schaffhausen – Zurich – Zug – Schwyz – Altdorf
A5	Yverdon – Neuchâtel – Biel – Solothurn
A6	Biel – Bern – Thun – Spiez
A7	Winterthur – Kreuzlingen – German border
A8	Spiez – Interlaken – (Brünig Pass) – Lucerne
A9	French border – Lausanne – Montreux – Martigny – Sion – Brig
A12	Vevey – Fribourg – Bern
A13	St Margrethen – Chur – San Bernardino Tunnel – Bellinzona
A14	Lucerne – A4
A16	French border – Delémont – Biel
A51	Zurich – Zurich airport – Bülach
A53	Zurich – Rapperswil – A3

Did you know?
The A1 is Switzerland's longest motorway and its first 8km opened in May 1962 between Bern Wankdorf and Schönbühl. The oldest section of Swiss motorway is the A2 between Lucerne and Horw, opened in 1955.

Swiss Football Cup

Most cup victories
18 Grasshopper Club Zurich
12 FC Sion
11 FC Basel
9   Lausanne-Sports
7   FC Zurich, Servette FC
6   BSC Young Boys, FC La Chaux-de-Fonds
3   FC Lugano
2   FC Luzern
1   FC Aarau, FC Grenchen, FC St Gallen, FC Wil,
    Urania-Genève-Sport, Young Fellows Zurich

First cup final:
1926 at the Letzigrund stadium in Zurich
Grasshopper Club Zurich beat FC Bern 2:1

Most wins in a row:
Grasshopper Club Zurich - four from 1940-43

Most finals contested:
Grasshopper Club Zurich – 30, 18 won, 12 lost

Most doubles (League and Cup):
Grasshopper Club Zurich – eight in
1927, 1937, 1942, 1943, 1952, 1956, 1983, 1990.

Highest scoring finals:

1935	Lausanne-Sports 10:0 Nordstern Basel	
1937	Grasshopper Club Zurich 10:0 Lausanne-Sports	

Winners & runners-up since 2000:

2000	FC Zurich	Lausanne-Sports	2:2 (5:2 after penalties)
2001	Servette FC	Yverdon-Sport	3-0
2002	FC Basel	Grasshopper Club	2:1
2003	FC Basel	Neuchâtel Xamax	6:0
2004	FC Wil	Grasshopper Club	3:2
2005	FC Zurich	FC Luzern	3:1
2006	FC Sion	BSC Young Boys	1:1 (5:3 after penalties)
2007	FC Basel	FC Luzern	1:0
2008	FC Basel	AC Bellinzona	4:1
2009	FC Sion	BSC Young Boys	3:2
2010	FC Basel	Lausanne-Sports	6:0
2011	FC Sion	Neuchâtel Xamax	2:0
2012	FC Basel	FC Luzern	1:1 (5:3 after penalties)

Cantonal Capitals by Height

		metres			metres
Appenzell	AI	775	Lucerne	LU	436
Herisau	AR	771	Neuchâtel	NE	435
St Gallen	SG	670	Solothurn	SO	432
Fribourg	FR	629	Zug	ZG	425
Chur	GR	595	Delémont	JU	413
Bern	BE	540	Zurich	ZH	406
Schwyz	SZ	516	Frauenfeld	TG	405
Sion	VS	491	Schaffhausen	SH	403
Glarus	GL	472	Geneva	GE	375
Sarnen	OW	471	Aarau	AG	371
Altdorf	UR	458	Liestal	BL	327
Stans	NW	452	Basel	BS	244
Lausanne	VD	447	Bellinzona	TI	227

Did you know?

Bern is the capital of both its canton and the country (although technically it is called the Federal City, rather than the national capital). It is the third-highest European capital after Andorra la Vella (1023m) and Madrid (667m).

A Year of Weddings

From 2000 to 2010 inclusive 445,726 weddings took place in Switzerland. August was the most popular month overall, with a total of 56,076 marriages.

August	12.58%	April	7.45%
June	11.86%	March	6.42%
May	11.55%	December	5.62%
September	11.07%	February	5.47%
July	10.61%	November	4.97%
October	7.55%	January	4.84%

UNESCO Heritage Sites

The first Swiss sites were added to the Unesco World Heritage List in 1983.

Cultural Sites

1983 Abbey & library in St Gallen

1983 Convent of St John in Müstair (GR)

1983 Old City of Bern

2000 Bellinzona castles, walls and ramparts (TI)

2007 Lavaux Terrace Vineyards (VD)

2008 Rhaetian Railway (Albula & Bernina sections, GR)

2009 La Chaux-de-Fonds & Le Locle (NE)

2011 Prehistoric pile dwellings (56 of 111 sites around the Alps)

Natural sites

2001 Swiss Alps Jungfrau-Aletsch (BE & VS)

2003 Monte San Giorgio (TI)

2008 Swiss Tectonic Area Sardona (GL, GR & SG)

Did you know?
Maurice Koechlin from Zurich was the engineer who had the original design idea for a metal tower in Paris. It was eventually named after the head of the engineering firm where Koechlin worked, Gustav Eiffel.

Speed Limits

Limits		Exceptions	
50	Built-up areas	80	Vehicles with a trailer or spike tyres
80	Outside built-up areas except on major roads	60	Commercial tractors
		40	When towing
		40	Agricultural tractors
100	Major roads	30	Agricultural vehicles and when towing agricultural trailers
120	Motorways	30	Vehicles with solid rubber or metal tyres
		5	When reversing

Interesting Road Rules

Some of the rules taken from the guidebook for passing the theory part of the Swiss driving test.

- **Rule 381** If there are children in the vicinity, who are not paying attention to the traffic, slow down and stop if necessary. Use the horn! Children are unpredictable, so are animals
- **Rule 528** Traffic lights are round: red is above, green is below, and amber may be placed in the middle
- **Rule 719** Do not steal a parking space from another waiting driver
- **Rule 864** It is forbidden to board, exit or lean out of moving vehicles and trams
- **Rule 865** Drivers and passengers may not throw or hold objects out of vehicles, except during processions on closed roads
- **Rule 891** Drivers must never inconvenience other road users or nearby residents by making noise, or causing smoke, dust or fumes. When possible animals should not be frightened
- **Rule 892** It is prohibited to use loudspeakers on vehicles
- **Rule 893** Drivers, passengers and other personnel must avoid making noise in residential or recreation areas, and at night
- **Rule 894** It is prohibited to: bang doors, bonnets, boots, etc., accelerate too fast, especially when moving off, come and go unnecessarily (especially in residential areas), disturb others by playing radios, tape-recorders, etc. which are carried or built into the vehicle
- **Rule 982** Incorrigible drivers will have their licences withdrawn permanently

Did you know?

Foreign residents must exchange their national driving licence for a Swiss one within one year of arrival. If not, they must take the Swiss driving test.

The Swiss Air-Rescuers

Swiss Air-Rescue, or Rega, was founded by Dr Rudolf Bucher on 27 April 1952. More than just a mountain rescue service, it provides fast medical assistance by air – both in Switzerland and abroad. It has 2.3 million patrons, 319 staff, 17 helicopters and 3 ambulance jets.

Total rescue missions	14,240
Helicopter	10,797
Aircraft	1,052
Other (eg ambulance)	2,391
Primary types of incident	
Illness	1,692
Winter sports accidents	1,581
Road accidents	924
Occupational accidents	878
Mountain accidents	765
Sports accidents	396
Aviation accidents	128
Avalanche	77

**Main reasons for
helicopter missions**

Head injury	1,994
Heart/circulatory problems	1,666
Back injury	636
Dead people	361
Newborn babies	224

Missions abroad

Medical assistance by phone	1,276
Repatriation by ambulance jet	698
Repatriation by scheduled flight	326

(All figures from 2011)

Did you know?

A Rega annual family membership also gives a Swiss farmer protection for his cows when they are up in the high pastures in summer. Injured, sick or dead cows are rescued by air and brought down to lower levels for treatment. On average 1,000 missions for cows are flown each year.

National Population Change

1291	800,000
1400	600,000
1500	800,000
1600	900,000
1700	1,200,000
1800	1,664,832
1850 **(first official census)**	**2,392,740**
1875	2,733,487
1900	3,318,985
1925	3,989,227
1950	4,717,200
1960	5,360,153
1970	6,193,064
1980	6,335,243
1990	6,750,693
2000	7,204,055
2010	7,870,100

Before 1800 the figures are academic estimates for the area that is now modern Switzerland.

Did you know?
Switzerland has 12,553km² of woodland, with four cantons –
Graubünden, Bern, Ticino and Vaud – containing more than half
of all Swiss woods. Coniferous trees make up over two-thirds, and
the most common types of tree overall are spruce (45%), beech
(18%) and silver fir (15%).

Two Foreign Lands

Within Switzerland's borders are two tiny foreign enclaves, or communities cut off from their own countries. One belongs to Germany, the other to Italy but both are surrounded by Switzerland.

Büsingen am Hochrhein   German district: Konstanz
Population: 1,396   Area: 7.62 km²
Swiss postcode: 8238   German postcode: 78266
Phone prefixes: +41 52 (Swiss) or +49 7734 (German)
Surrounding canton: Schaffhausen (and River Rhine)

Campione d'Italia   Italian district: Como
Population: 2,267   Area: 1.6 km²
Swiss postcode: 6911   Italian postcode: 22060
Phone prefix: +41 91 (Swiss)
Surrounding canton: Ticino (and Lake Lugano)

In comparison, the Principality of Monaco is 2.02 km² with a population of 35,881

Swiss Watch Brands

The Swiss watch industry started in Geneva in the 16th century. Today there are 205 Swiss watch brands and 40,000 employees in Switzerland.

Ten of the oldest		Ten of the most famous	
Blancpain	1735	Omega	1848
Favre-Leuba	1737	Tissot	1853
Vacheron Constantin	1755	Tag Heuer	1860
Girard-Perregaux	1791	Zenith	1865
ETA	1793	IWC	1868
Baume et Mercier	1830	Movado	1881
Longines	1832	Breitling	1884
LeCoultre	1833	Rolex	1908
Invicta	1837	Mondaine	1951
Patek Philippe	1839	Swatch	1983

Lucerne's City Wall Towers

The Musegg Wall around Lucerne was built in 1388 and nine towers still stand along its length.

	Height
Nölli	28m
Männli	33m
Luegisland	52.6m
Wacht	44m
Zyt	31m
Schirme	27.5m
Pulver	27.5m
Allenwinden	27.5m
Dächli	27.35m

Did you know?
The oldest working clock in Lucerne is housed in the Zyt Tower. It was built in 1535 and is allowed to chime one minute before all the other clocks in Lucerne.

Some Swiss Records

Longest international tram ride: Line 10 with 40 stops through Basel, Solothurn and France, 25.9km and 63 minutes.

Europe's **largest** kosher hotel: Scoul Palace in Graubünden with 120 rooms.

World's **highest** train usage: 2,258km per person per year.

Longest time holding a breath underwater: Swiss diver Peter Colat with 21 minutes, 33 seconds, set on 17 September 2011.

World's **largest** chalet: the Grand Chalet at Rossinière (VD). Built in 1754, it is 19.5m high, has 113 windows and more than 700 m^3 of pine was used in its construction.

First non-stop flight around the world in a balloon, by Bertrand Piccard in 1999.

World's **longest** staircase: 11,674 stairs alongside the line climbing up Niesen. Total length is 3,499m and the **fastest** time to climb, 1 hour 3 minutes 7 seconds.

World's **smallest** bar (with a permanent licence): the 'Smallest Whisky Bar on Earth' in Santa Maria (GR), with a floor area of 8.53m^2.

Europe's **largest** clock face in Aarau (AG) train station, with a diameter of 9 metres.

World's **deepest** dive: 10,911m to the bottom of the Marianas Trench, achieved by Jacques Piccard in 1960.

Europe's **highest** permanently-inhabited village: Juf (GR) at an altitude of 2126m.

Lausanne is the **smallest** city in the world to have a metro and the only city in Switzerland with one.

Europe's **highest** cable-car station: Klein Matterhorn (VS) at an altitude of 3883m.

Switzerland in the World Cup

Switzerland has qualified for football's World Cup Finals nine times.

Best results:

1934	Quarter final (lost 3-2 to Czechoslovakia)
1938	Quarter final (lost 2-0 to Hungary)
1954	Quarter final (lost 7-5 to Austria)

Eliminated in group stage: 1950, 1962, 1966, 2010
Eliminated in last 16: 1994, 2006

World Cup host

Switzerland hosted the fifth World Cup finals in 1954. It was the highest-scoring World Cup finals ever, with an average of 5.38 goals per match (140 goals in 26 matches), including the highest-scoring match, Switzerland vs Austria quarter-final; the Swiss lost 5-7. West Germany won the final at Wankdorf Stadium in Bern on 4 July 1954. Beating the favourites Hungary 3-2 became known as the 'Miracle of Bern'.

Locations used:

Basel	St Jakob Stadium (Semi Final)
Bern	Wankdorf Stadium (Final)
Geneva	Stade des Charmilles
Lausanne	Stade Olympique de la Pontaise (Semi Final)
Lugano	Stadio Comunale Cornaredo
Zurich	Hardturm Stadium

Did you know?

In 2006, Switzerland was eliminated without conceding a goal in normal play but also without scoring once in the penalty shoot-out against Ukraine. Switzerland also holds the record for most consecutive minutes played without conceding a goal (9 hours & 19 minutes), set in the 2006 & 2010 World Cup finals.

Swiss Funiculars

Europe's first public funicular was 'La Ficelle', built in 1877 to link Lausanne and Ouchy. In 1958 it was replaced with a cog railway.

Date

1879	Giessbach	BE
1885	Marzili	BE
1886	Lugano Stazione	TI
1887	Biel-Magglingen	BE
1887	Bürgenstock	NW
1888	San Salvatore	TI
1889	Polybahn	ZH
1893	Stanserhorn	NW
1898	Bienne-Evilard	BE
1899	Fribourg	FR
1899	Gurten	BE
1899	Reichenbach Falls	BE
1902	Sonnenberg	LU
1905	Madonna del Sasso	TI
1906	Heimwehfluh	BE
1908	Monte Brè I	TI
1908	Harder Kulm	BE
1910	Les Avants	VD
1910	Niesen	BE
1912	Monte Brè II	TI

Did you know?
Europe's longest funicular is in Valais, linking Sierre with Crans-Montana. It is 4,191m long and covers a height difference of 927m with a journey time of 12 minutes.

Most Common Causes of Death

	Men	Women	Total
Cardiovascular disease	9,872	12,356	22,228
Cardiopathy: all types	7,744	9,281	17,025
Cerbrovascular disease	1,511	2,401	3,912
Cancer	8,824	7,238	16,062
Large intestine	623	549	1,172
Lungs	1,922	1,037	2,959
Breast	12	1,439	1,451
Dementia	1,375	3,344	4,719
Respiratory tract diseases	2,128	1,963	4,091
Accidents & trauma	2,219	1,361	3,580
Suicides	827	278	1,105
Diabetes mellitus	667	752	1,419
Infectious diseases	331	345	676
Alcoholic liver cirrhosis	311	162	473
All causes of death	30,034	32,442	62,476

Did you know?

The last witch to be executed in Europe was Anna Göldi from Canton Glarus. She was beheaded on 13 June 1782 after being found guilty of poisoning a child. In 2008 the cantonal government exonerated her.

Riding the Rack Railways

Europe's first mountain train, or rack railway, was built in Switzerland to take passengers up the Rigi in 1871. There followed a forty-year building craze that resulted in these famous rack (or cog-wheel) railways:

	Opened	Max Height
Rigi (LU-SZ)	21 May 1871	1797m
Pilatus (LU)	4 June 1889	2132m
Monte Generoso (TI)	4 June 1890	1704m
Brienzer Rothorn (BE)	17 June 1892	2244m
Rochers-de-Naye (VD)	16 September 1892	2042m
Schynige Platte (BE)	14 June 1893	1967m
Kleine Scheidegg (BE)	20 June 1893	2061m
Rorschach-Heiden (SG-AR)	3 September 1875	810m
Visp-Zermatt (VS)	18 July 1891	1605m
Gornergrat (VS)	20 August 1898	3089m
Aigle-Leysin (VD)	5 May 1900	1450m
Mont-Blanc Express[1] (VS)	20 August 1906	1224m
St-Bernard Express[2] (VS)	27 August 1910	902m
Jungfraujoch (BE)	1 August 1912	3454m

[1]Until 1990 called the Martigny-Châtelard line
[2]Until 1990 called the Martigny-Orsières line

Did you know?
The world's steepest rack railway runs from Alpnachstad up to the summit of Pilatus, with a maximum gradient of 48%.

Population Density

The least crowded canton, Graubünden, has a density similar to Kyrgyzstan or Vermont. Not surprisingly, Basel-Stadt is the most crowded canton, with a population density comparable to Greater London.

Density (per km²)		Density (per km²)	
Graubünden	27.1	Neuchâtel	214.3
Uri	32.9	Appenzell AR	218.3
Glarus	56.3	Vaud	222.1
Valais	59.9	St Gallen	236.3
Obwalden	72.5	Thurgau	250.7
Jura	83.5	Lucerne	252.8
Appenzell AI	90.9	Schaffhausen	255.8
Ticino	118.7	Solothurn	322.9
Nidwalden	148.6	Aargau	435.6
Schwyz	161.6	Zug	473.6
Bern	164.4	Basel-Land	530.2
Fribourg	166.7	Zurich	794.2
Switzerland	**190.6**	Geneva	1620.8
Neuchâtel	214.3	Basel-Stadt	4985.2

Did you know?

The Swiss city with the highest population density is Geneva with 11,805 people per km², followed by Basel (6,815), Zurich (4,242) and Lausanne (3,092). No wonder flats are so expensive in Geneva.

The White Death

The ten worst single Swiss avalanches.

Deaths	Location	Date
84	Obergesteln (VS)	18 Februry 1870
64	Rueras (GR)	6 February 1749
53	Leukerbad (VS)	17 January 1719
52	Biel/Selkingen (VS)	17 January 1827
36	Ftan (GR)	8 February 1720
34	Bosco (GR)	21 February 1695
30	Reckingen (VS)	24 February 1970
29	Bedretto (VS)	7 January 1863
25	Rueras (GR)	6 March 1817
25	Selva (GR)	13 December 1808

A Multilingual Country

Languages by percentage of the population:

National languages

German	63.7%	Italian	6.5%
French	20.4%	Romansh	0.5%

Non-national languages 9%

Of which:	Serbo-Croat	1.4%	Arabic	0.2%
	Albanian	1.3%	Dutch	0.2%
	Portuguese	1.2%	Chinese	0.1%
	Spanish	1.1%	Kurdish	0.1%
	English	1.0%	Macedonian	0.1%
	Turkish	0.6%	Russian	0.1%
	Tamil	0.3%	Thai	0.1%

Reading the News

The main Swiss newspapers and magazines

Swiss weekly magazines

German	Sales
Coop Zeitung	(free) 1,770,380
Migros-Magazin	(free) 1,558,918
Beobachter	301,236
Schweizer Illustrierte	198,660
NZZ Folio	197,728
Schweizer Familie	186,588
Tele	145,939
TV-Star	130,537
Reader's Digest Schweiz	94,049
Die Weltwoche	77,800

French	
Coopération	(free) 601,673
Migros Magazine	(free) 505,869
Télé Top Matin	175,644
Fémina	175,077
TV8	87,699
L'Illustré	86,264

Italian	
Cooperazione	(free) 123,501
Azione (Migros)	(free) 98,600
TicinoSette	70,634

German newspapers	Daily sales
20 Minuten	(free) 496,205
Blick am Abend	(free) 321,095
Blick	208,360
Tages-Anzeiger	195,618
Aargauer Zeitung	178,854
Berner Zeitung	174,162
Neue Zürcher Zeitung (NZZ)	132,670
Südostschweiz	122,470
Neue Luzerner Zeitung	121,371
St Galler Tagblatt	118,420
Basler Zeitung	77,619
Der Bund	50,231
Sonntags-Blick	230,180
Sonntags Zeitung	182,129
Der Sonntag	158,115
NZZ am Sonntag	130,133

French	
20 Minutes	(free) 203,407
24 Heures	75,796
Le Matin	57,107
Le Temps	42,433
La Liberté	39,086
Le Matin dimanche	175,951

Italian	
Corriere del Ticino	36,274
La Regione	32,379

Romansh	
La Quotidiana	5,000

National Cycling Routes

Alongside the 53 designated regional and 45 local routes are 9 national ones.

| Route 1 | **Rhone** | 345km (26km unsurfaced), 8 sections |

Andermatt – Oberwald – Brig – Sierre – Martigny – Montreux – Morges – Geneva

| Route 2 | **Rhine** | 430km (68km unsurfaced), 9 sections |

Andermatt – Chur – Buchs – Kreuzlingen – Schaffhausen – Zurzach – Basel

| Route 3 | **North-South** | 365km (30km unsurfaced), 8 sections |

Basel – Aarau – Lucerne – Flüelen – Andermatt – Airolo – Bellinzona – Chiasso

| Route 4 | **Alpine Panorama** | 485km (10km unsurfaced), 8 sections |

St Margrethen – Appenzell – Glarus – Sörenberg – Thun – Fribourg – Aigle

Route 5 **Mittelland** 370km (85km unsurfaced), 7 sections

Romanshorn – Wil – Kloten – Aarau – Solothurn – Ins – Yverdon – Lausanne

Route 6 **Graubünden**

Branch 1: 128km (25km unsurfaced), 3 sections

Chur – Thusis – Splügen – San Bernadino – Bellinzona

Branch 2: 152km (55km unsurfaced), 4 sections

Chur – Thusis – Bergün – Zernez – Martina

Route 7 **Jura** 280km (14km unsurfaced), 6 sections

Basel – Courgenay – La Chaux-de-Fonds – Fleurier – Vallorbe – Nyon

Route 8 **Aare** 305km (64km unsurfaced), 7 sections

Oberwald – Meiringen – Spiez – Bern – Biel – Solothurn – Aarau – Koblenz

Route 9 **Lakes** 505km (64km unsurfaced), 10 sections

Montreux – Gstaad – Spiez – Meiringen – Zug – Einsiedeln – Buchs – Rorschach

Tour de Suisse Winners

The Tour de Suisse bike race first took place in August-September 1933, and was won by Max Bulla from Austria. The record number of wins by one cyclist is four (Pasquale Fornara, Italy, between 1952 and 1958).

Winners since 2000

2000	Oskar Camenzind	Switzerland
2001	Lance Armstrong	USA
2002	Alex Zülle	Switzerland
2003	Alexandre Vinokourov	Kazakhstan
2004	Jan Ullrich	Germany
2005	Aitor Gonzalez	Spain
2006	Jan Ullrich	Germany
2007	Vladimir Karpets	Russia
2008	Roman Kreuziger	Czech Republic
2009	Fabian Cancellara	Switzerland
2010	Fränk Schleck	Luxembourg
2011	Levi Leipheimer	USA

Did you know?

Switzerland holds the record for the most wins by one country – 23. Three of those victories were from one of the most famous Swiss cyclists, Ferdi Kübler, who triumphed on home soil in 1942, 1948 and 1951.

Most Common Surnames

Müller is by far the most common family name in Switzerland, with 25,870 entries in the phone book covering 553 different postcodes.

German		French	Italian
Müller	Huber	Martin	Bernasconi
Meier	Schneider	Favre	Rossi
Schmid	Meyer	Rey	Ferrari
Keller	Steiner	Rochat	Bianchi
Weber	Fischer		

Not Born Swiss

Some famous 'Swiss' people who were not Swiss at birth

Albert Einstein	scientist	Germany
Nicolas Hayek	watchmaker	Lebanon
Herman Hesse	author	Germany
Martina Hingis	tennis player	Czechoslovakia
Henri Nestlé	industrialist	Germany
Meret Oppenheim	artist	Germany
Niki de Saint Phalle	artists	France
Maximilian Schell	actor	Austria
Madame Tussaud	waxworker	France
Peter Ustinov	actor	United Kingdom

The artist Paul Klee was born in Münchenbuchsee (BE) but had German nationality, thanks to his father. His application for Swiss citizenship would have been approved on 5 July 1940 but he died on 29 June.

Protected Products

Switzerland has two ways of protecting products made in specific areas of the country: AOC (Appellation d'Origine Contrôlée) and IGP (Indication Géographique Protégée).

AOC products

Abricotine	Apricot liqueur	Valais
Berner Alpkäse	Cheese	Bern
Berner Hobelkäse	Cheese	Bern
Bloder-Sauerkäse	Cheese	St Gallen
Cardon épineux genevois	Vegetable	Geneva
Damassine	Plum liqueur	Jura
Emmentaler	Cheese	11 cantons, not just Bern
L'Etivaz	Cheese	Vaud
Eau-de-vie de poire du Valais	Pear liqueur	Valais
Formaggio d'Alpe Ticinese	Cheese	Ticino
Le Gruyère	Cheese	5 cantons, not just Fribourg
Munder Safran	Spice	Valais
Poire à Botzi	Fruit	Fribourg

Rheintaler Ribelmais	Corn flour	St Gallen & Graubünden
Sbrinz	Cheese	Central Switzerland
Tête de Moine	Cheese	Jura & Bern
Vacherin Fribourgeois	Cheese	Fribourg
Vacherin Mont d'Or	Cheese	Vaud
Raclette du Valais	Cheese	Valais
Walliser Roggenbrot	Bread	Valais

IGP products

Bündnerfleisch	Cured meat	Graubünden
Longeole	Sausage	Geneva
Saucisse d'Ajoie	Sausage	Jura
Saucisse au choux vaudoise	Sausage	Vaud
Saucisse neuchâteloise	Sausage	Neuchâtel
St Galler Bratwurst	Sausage	St Gallen
Saucisson vaudois	Sausage	Vaud
Walliser Trockenfleisch	Cured meat	Valais

Schwinger Kings

The Eidgenössischer Schwingerverband (ESV) or Swiss Wrestling Association was founded on 11 March 1895 in Bern and today has over 50,000 members. Every three years the Schwinger King is crowned at the Eidgenössisches Schwing- and Älplerfest, which moves location each time.

Winners since 1945

1948	Lucerne	Peter Vogt (Muttenz, BL)
1950	Grenchen	No Schwinger King
1953	Winterthur	Walter Flach (Hinwil, ZH)
1956	Thun	Eugen Holzherr (Basel)
1958	Freiburg	Max Widmer (Oftringen, AG)
1961	Zug	Karl Meli (Winterthur, ZH)
1964	Aarau	Karl Meli (Winterthur, ZH)
1966	Frauenfeld	Ruedi Hunsperger (Habstetten, BE)

1969	Biel/Bienne	Ruedi Hunsperger (Habstetten, BE)
1972	La Chaux-de-Fonds	David Roschi (Oberwil im Simmental, BE)
1974	Schwyz	Ruedi Hunsperger (Habstetten, BE)
1977	Basel	Arnold Ehrensberger (Winterthur, ZH)
1980	St. Gallen	Ernst Schläpfer (Herisau, AR)
1983	Langenthal	Ernst Schläpfer (Herisau, AR)
1986	Sion	Heinrich Knüsel (Abtwil, AG)
1989	Stans	Adrian Käser (Alchenstorf, BE)*
1992	Olten	Silvio Rüfenacht (Hasle-Rüegsau, BE)
1995	Chur	Thomas Sutter (Appenzell)
1998	Bern	Jörg Abderhalden (Alt St. Johann & Nesslau, SG)
2001	Nyon	Arnold Forrer (Stein, AR)
2004	Lucerne	Jörg Abderhalden (Alt St. Johann & Nesslau, SG)
2007	Aarau	Jörg Abderhalden (Alt St. Johann & Nesslau, SG)
2010	Frauenfeld	Kilian Wenger (Horboden, BE)

*youngest ever king of the Schwingers, aged 18

Did you know?

Schwingen takes place in an outdoor ring of sawdust with both combatants wearing baggy shorts (made from sacking) over their clothes. There are five main throws – Brienzer, Bur, Hüfter, Kurz and Übersprung – all with the aim of getting the opponent's shoulders to touch the ground, while still having at least one hand on his over-sized shorts. The winner traditionally brushes the sawdust off the loser's back.

Important National Referendum Results

The Yes victories…

	Date	Yes %
Federal constitution	12.9.1848	72.8
New constitution	19.4.1874	63.2
Factory law (11-hour day & Sundays off)	21.10.1877	51.5
Popular initiative introduced	5.7.1891	60.3
Swiss Federal Railways (SBB / CFF / FFS) created	20.2.1898	67.9
Absinthe banned	5.7.1908	63.5
Proportional representation	13.10.1918	66.8
League of Nations entry	16.5.1920	56.3
Romansh as the fourth national language	20.2.1938	91.6
AHV (state pensions)	6.7.1947	80.0
Votes for women	7.2.1971	65.7
Free Trade agreement with the EEC	3.12.1972	72.5

Jura as the 23rd canton	24.9.1978	82.3
Compulsory seatbelts in front seats	30.11.1981	51.6
Equal rights for men and women	14.6.1981	60.3
Motorway tax sticker introduced	26.2.1984	53.0
NEAT tunnels under the Alps	27.9.1992	63.6
New constitution	18.4.1999	59.2
Bilateral I agreements with EU	21.5.2000	67.2
UN membership	3.2.2002	54.6
Abortion within 12 weeks legalised	2.6.2002	72.2
Same-sex civil partnerships	5.6.2005	58.0
Schengen & Dublin agreements	5.6.2005	54.6
Ban on new minarets	29.11.2009	57.5
Deportation of foreign criminals	28.11.2010	52.3

…and some notable No's

	Date	Yes %
Proportional representation	4.11.1900	40.9
Proportional representation	23.10.1910	47.5
AHV (state pensions)	6.12.1931	39.7
Votes for women	1.2.1959	33.1
10% limit on foreign population	7.6.1970	46.0
12% limit on foreign population	20.10.1974	34.2
UN membership	16.3.1986	24.3
Switzerland without an army	26.11.1989	35.6
EEA membership	6.12.1992	49.7
EU entry	4.3.2001	23.2
Banning the export of weapons	29.11.2009	31.8

Cheese Consumption

The Swiss love Swiss cheese. 73% of the cheese eaten in Switzerland is Swiss made. Most popular is fresh cheese (such as mozzarella, mascarpone, quark and cream cheese) which accounts for a third of all cheese consumed.

Most popular sorts	Grams*
Mozzarella	2,470
Le Gruyère AOC	1,700
Swiss Raclette	1,280
Emmentaler AOC	730
Parmesan	700
Ready-made fondue	490
Appenzeller	400
Tilsiter	350
Vacherin Fribourgeois AOC	280
Walliser Raclette AOC	270
Sbrinz AOC	170

*All consumption figures are per person per year.

Top Ten Cheese-Eating Countries

Even though the Swiss eat an awful lot of cheese – an average of 21.5kg each per year – they are easily beaten by those champion cheese-eaters, the French. As for all those great British cheeses, it clearly isn't the Brits who are eating them.

	Kilos*
France	26.1
Iceland	25.4
Germany	22.6
Switzerland	21.5
Netherlands	21.0
Italy	20.9
Finland	20.7
Turkey	19.4
Sweden	18.9
Czech Republic	16.7
EU average	16.6
USA	14.8
UK	10.9

*All consumption figures are per person per year.

The Fields of Switzerland

Annual production for different crops.

Grains		tonnes
	Wheat	507,470
	Barley	174,113
	Corn	143,502
	Rapeseed	67,900
	Triticale*	58,332
	Spelt	16,093
	Dried peas	14,537
	Rye	13,708
	Sunflowers	10,600
	Oats	8,932

Vegetables		tonnes
	Sugar beet	1,719,710
	Potatoes	517,000
	Lettuce	70,543
	Carrots	69,874
	Tomatoes	34,450
	Cabbages	34,253
	Onions	33,648
	Spinach	16,997
	Leeks	10,818
	Cucumbers	9,513

Fruit		tonnes
	Apples	252,086
	Pears	73,884
	Cherries	10,210
	Apricots	9,450
	Strawberries	7,018
	Plums	6,830
	Raspberries	1,714
	Quinces	614
	Kiwi	548
	Currants	495

*wheat-rye hybrid

Characters in Heidi

From the original German text of this famous story by Johanna Spyri, published in 1880-81

Heidi	an orphan girl
Dete	her maternal aunt
Adelheid	her dead mother
Tobias	her dead father
Alpöhi	her paternal grandfather
Barbel	Dete's friend
Peter	a goatherd
Brigitte	his mother
Grossmutter	his grandmother
Klara Sesemann	an invalid girl in Frankfurt
Herr Sesemann	her rich father
Frau Sesemann	her grandmother
Dr Classen	her doctor
Herr Kandidat	her tutor
Fräulein Rottenmeier	the Sesemann's housekeeper
Johann	the Sesemann's coachman
Sebastian	the Sesemann's servant
Tinette	the Sesemann's maid

A poor organ player
A baker
A pastor
A teacher

Goats	Bärli, Distelfink, Schnecke, Schneehöppli, Schwänli, Türk

Baby Names

Most popular names given to babies in 2010: 39,179 girls and 41,111 boys born.

German

Boys	Girls
Noah	Lena
Luca	Mia
Leon	Lara
Jonas	Alina
David	Lea
Nico	Laura
Jan	Sara
Levin	Anna
Leandro	Leonie
Julian	Julia

French

Boys	Girls
Nathan	Emma
Gabriel	Léa
Luca	Lara
Noah	Eva
Maxime	Emilie
Nolan	Camille
Lucas	Anaïs
Louis	Zoé
Arthur	Chloé
Thomas	Clara

Italian

Boys	Girls
Mattia	Giulia
Alessandro	Sofia
Andrea	Noemi
Leonardo	Emma
Matteo	Martina
Lorenzo	Alice

Romansh

Boys	Girls
Laurin	Lea
Leandro	Mara
Silvan	Fiona
Simon	Iris
Gian	Kim
Joel	Ladina

Did you know?

Noah was the most popular boys' name in Cantons Aargau, Zurich, Solothurn and St Gallen. Lena was the favourite girls' name in Cantons Bern, Lucerne, Nidwalden, Solothurn, St Gallen and Zurich.

Cantonal Government

The 26 cantonal legislatures, or parliaments, have 2,608 seats between them - roughly 1 seat for every 3,000 inhabitants.

Canton	Seats	Inhabitants per seat
Appenzell AI	49	320
Uri	64	553
Glarus	60	643
Obwalden	55	647
Nidwalden	60	684
Appenzell AR	65	816
Jura	60	1,167
Schaffhausen	60	1,273
Zug	80	1,414
Schwyz	100	1,467
Neuchâtel	115	1,496
Graubünden	120	1,605
Basel-Stadt	100	1,850
Thurgau	130	1,911
Valais	130	2,405
Fribourg	110	2,532
Solothurn	100	2,553
Basel-Land	90	3,049
Lucerne	120	3,147
Ticino	90	3,708
St Gallen	120	3,991
Aargau	140	4,368
Geneva	100	4,577
Vaud	150	4,755
Bern	160	6,124
Zurich	180	7,628

Every canton has a multi-member governing council.

Five-member councils: Aargau, Basel-Land, Glarus, Graubünden, Jura, Lucerne, Neuchâtel, Obwalden, Schaffhausen, Solothurn, Thurgau, Ticino, Valais.

Seven-member councils: Appenzell AI, Appenzell AR, Basel-Stadt, Bern, Fribourg, Geneva, Nidwalden, Schwyz, St Gallen, Uri, Vaud, Zug, Zurich

Swiss Death Tolls in Single Events

Deaths	Location	Date
457	Landslide, Goldau (SZ)	2.9.1806
114	Landslide, Elm (GL)	11.9.1881
88	Glacier collapse, Mattmark (VS)	30.8.1965
80	Swissair crash, Dürrenasch (AG)	4.9.1963
71	Train crash, Münchenstein (BL)	14.6.1891
63	Flood, Küsnacht (ZH)	8.7.1778
63	Fire in Hauenstein Tunnel	28.5.1857
47	Swissair bomb, Zurich	21.2.1970
41	Swissair crash, Halifax, Canada	3.9.1998
40	Wartime bombing, Schaffhausen	1.4.1944
36	Sata plane crash in Madeira	18.12.1977
36	Terrorist massacre, Luxor, Egypt	17.11.1997
25	Flood in Lötschberg Tunnel	24.7.1908
24	Train derailment, Colombier (NE)	22.3.1871
15	Gun massacre, Zug	27.9.2001
15	Train crash, Bellinzona	23.4.1924
13	Army shooting of protestors, Geneva	9.11.1932
13	Landslide, Gondo (VS)	14.10.2000
12	Swissair crash, Tuttlingen, Germany	27.7.1934
9	Wartime bombing, Stein am Rhein	22.2.1945

Did you know?

The last war fought on Swiss soil was the Sonderbund civil war of November 1847. Total death toll was 98 (mostly from the Federal forces, with 74 dead), which is higher than the number of Swiss deaths in World War II. Switzerland was neutral in that war but was bombed (mistakenly) on more than one occasion.

Top Ten Chocolate-Eating Countries

Kg per head per year

Switzerland	11.9
Germany	11.3
UK	10.9
Norway	9.6
Denmark	7.4
Finland	6.8
France	6.4
Sweden	6.1
USA	5.2
Belgium	5.0

Did you know?

About 94,000 tonnes of chocolate is consumed each year in Switzerland. Of that, 70% is milk, 25% dark and only 5% white.

Ten Swiss Chocolate Brands

Cailler	1819	Frey	1887
Suchard	1826	Toblerone	1908
Sprüngli	1845	Camille Bloch	1929
Maestrani	1852	Ragusa	1942
Lindt	1879	Alprose	1957

The Swiss French Connection

French speakers make up only 20.4% of the population but quite a few of them have made their mark in the world. So here are 20.4 famous Swiss people from the French-speaking part of the country.

Maurice Bavaud	failed assassin of Hitler
Louis Chevrolet	car maker
Le Corbusier	architect
Guillaume-Henri Dufour	general & co-founder of the Red Cross
Henri Dunant	humanitarian & co-founder of the Red Cross
Louis Favre	Gotthard Tunnel engineer
Albert Gallatin	first US Secretary of the Treasury
Henri Guisan	Second World War general
Jean-Paul Marat	French revolutionary
Georges de Mestral	inventor of Velcro
Claude Nicollier	only Swiss astronaut
Daniel Peter	inventor of milk chocolate
Bertrand Piccard	hot air balloonist
Jacques Piccard	underwater explorer
Marc Rosset	Olympic tennis gold medallist
Jean-Jacques Rousseau	philosopher
Philippe Senderos	footballer
Philippe Suchard	chocolate maker
Jean Tinguely	artist
Madame Tussaud	waxworker

And the 0.4? Jean Calvin – the religious reformer was French but is often mistaken for being Swiss. He lived and died in Geneva and was largely responsible for the Reformation becoming so strong in Switzerland.

Road Passes over 2000m

Umbrail	2501m	Graubünden – Italy
Nufenen	2478m	Ticino – Valais
Great St Bernard	2469m	Valais – Italy
Furka	2431m	Uri – Valais
Flüela	2383m	Graubünden
Bernina	2323m	Graubünden
Livigno	2315m	Graubünden – Italy
Albula	2312m	Graubünden
Julier	2284m	Graubünden
Susten	2224m	Bern – Uri
Grimsel	2165m	Bern – Valais
Ofenpass	2149m	Graubünden
Splügen	2113m	Graubünden – Italy
St Gotthard	2108m	Ticino – Uri
San Bernardino	2065m	Graubünden – Ticino
Oberalp	2044m	Graubünden – Uri
Simplon	2005m	Valais – Italy

Romansh – the Minority Language

Officially there are 35,000 Romansh speakers in Switzerland, or 0.5% of the population. Taking a wider definition of language use than the official census (ie those who use the language regularly at home, work or school) means the number of Romansh speakers is 60,500, or 0.8% of the whole population. Most of them live in Graubünden, the only canton where Romansh is an official language.

English	Sursilvan	Sutsilvan	Surmiran
I	jeu	jou	ia
cheese	caschiel	caschiel	caschiel
dog	tgaun	tgàn	tgang
easy	lev	leav	lev
eye	egl	îl	îgl
hard	dir	dir	deir
hour	ura	ura	oura
house	casa	tgeasa	tgesa
leg	comba	tgomba	tgomma
snow	neiv	nev	neiv

Romansh has five variations, known as idioms, and the official written version Rumantsch Grischun (RG), which was introduced in 1982. Sursilvan is the most widely-spoken idiom (52%) and Sutsilvan the least used (2%).

Did you know?
The community with the highest percentage of Romansh speakers is Vrin in the Surselva area. Of its 247 inhabitants, 95.6% use Romansh as their first language.

English	Puter	Vallader	RG
I	eau	eu	jau
cheese	chaschöl	chaschöl	chaschiel
dog	chaun	chan	chaun
easy	liger	leiv	lev
eye	ögl	ögl	egl
hard	dür	dür	dir
hour	ura	ura	ura
house	chesa	chasa	chasa
leg	chamma	chomma	chomma
snow	naiv	naiv	naiv

Presidents of Switzerland

Every December one member of the Federal Council is elected
President for a year. There have been 92 different holders of the
office since 1848.

First
Jonas Furrer   FDP ZH   1848

First from a party other than the FDP
Joseph Zemp   CVP LU   1895

First woman
Ruth Dreifuss   SP   GE   1999

Oldest president
Adolf Deucher   FDP TG   1909
(78 years, 10 months, 16 days)

Youngest president
Jakob Stämpfli   FDP BE   1856
(35 years, 10 months, 9 days)

Most terms
Karl Schenk	FDP	BE	1865, 1871, 1874, 1878, 1885, 1893
Emil Welti	FDP	AG	1869, 1872, 1876, 1880, 1884, 1891
Jonas Furrer	FDP	ZH	1848, 1849, 1852, 1855, 1858
Giuseppe Mottta	CVP	TI	1915, 1920, 1927, 1932, 1937

Died in office
Wilhelm Hertenstein (FDP, ZH) died on 27.11.1888, aged 63,
after a leg amputation.

Fridolin Anderwert (FDP, TG) was elected in 1880 to be President
for 1881 but committed suicide before taking office. Aged 52, he
shot himself on Christmas Day near Parliament in Bern.

Presidents by party

FDP	56	SVP	8
CVP	15	BDP	1
SP	11	LP	1

Presidents by canton

15 Zurich

13 Vaud

11 Bern

 6 Neuchâtel

 5 Aargau, Solothurn, St Gallen

 4 Geneva, Graubünden, Lucerne, Ticino

 2 Appenzell Ausserrhoden, Basel-Stadt,
   Fribourg, Thurgau, Valais, Zug

 1 Appenzell Innerrhoden, Basel-Land, Glarus, Obwalden

 0 Jura, Nidwalden, Schaffhausen, Schwyz and Uri

Presidents since 2000

2000	Adolf Ogi	SVP	BE
2001	Moritz Leuenberger	SP	ZH
2002	Kaspar Villiger	FDP	LU
2003	Pascal Couchepin	FDP	VS
2004	Joseph Deiss	CVP	FR
2005	Samuel Schmid	SVP*	BE
2006	Moritz Leuenberger	SP	ZH
2007	Micheline Calmy-Rey	SP	GE
2008	Pascal Couchepin	FDP	VS
2009	Hans-Rudolf Merz	FDP	AR
2010	Doris Leuthard	CVP	AG
2011	Micheline Calmy-Rey	SP	GE
2012	Eveline Widmer Schlumpf	BDP	GR

*In 2007 Samuel Schmid joined the BDP

Did you know?

Of the eight SVP presidents, all except one (Leon Schlumpf, GR) came from Canton Bern. The party's only Federal Councillor to leave office without being elected president was Christoph Blocher (ZH).

A Multilingual Gazetteer

Despite four national languages many place-names in Switzerland only have one version: Lugano, Montreux and Appenzell are all the same, whatever the language. But other names change so that it's possible to have four (or five with English) versions all in use. Here are some of the more interesting ones.

Places with a separate English name

English	German	French	Italian	Romansh
Geneva	Genf	Genève	Ginevra	Genevra
Rhine	Rhein	Rhin	Reno	Rain
St Gallen	Sankt Gallen	Saint-Gall	San Gallo	Son Gagl

Places where the German is used in English

German	French	Italian	Romansh
Chur	Coire	Coira	Cuira
Glarus	Glaris	Glarona	Glaruna
Graubünden	Grisons	Grigioni	Grischun
Nidwalden	Nidwald	Nidvaldo	Sutsilvania
Obwalden	Obwald	Obvaldo	Sursilvania
Schwyz	Schwytz	Svitto	Sviz
Solothurn	Soleure	Soletta	Soloturn

German- Romansh variations

German	Romansh
Davos	Tavau
Disentis	Mustér
Ilanz	Glion
Sankt Moritz	San Murezzan
Zürich	Turitg

German-French variations

German	French	German	French
Burgdorf	Berthoud	Münster	Moutier
Delsberg	Delémont	Murten	Morat
Düdingen	Guin	Neuenburg	Neuchâtel
Freiburg	Fribourg	Pruntrut	Porrentruy
Grenchen	Granges	Rütli	Grütli
Greyerz	Gruyères	Saanen	Gessenay
Ins	Anet	Siders	Sierre
Kerzers	Chiètres	Sitten	Sion
Leukerbad	Loèche-les-Bains	Wallis	Valais
Luzern	Lucerne	Waadt	Vaud
Matterhorn	Cervin		

Ten Tallest Dams

Grand Dixence is the tallest gravity dam in the world.

		Metres	Volume of water behind the dam
Grand Dixence	VS	285	401 million m^3
Mauvoisin	VS	250	211 million m^3
Luzzone	TI	225	108 million m^3
Contra (Verzasca)	TI	220	105 million m^3
Emosson	VS	180	227 million m^3
Zeuzier	VS	156	51 million m^3
Göscheneralp	UR	155	76 million m^3
Curnera	GR	153	41 million m^3
Zurvreila	GR	151	100 million m^3
Moiry	VS	148	78 million m^3

Did you know?
Hydroelectric power produces 55.6% of Swiss electricity, far more than the 39% from nuclear energy.

The Longest and Shortest Place Names

Longest name without hyphens or spaces:
Niederhelfenschwil (SG) 18 letters

Longest names with spaces:
Röthenbach bei Herzogenbuchsee (BE) 28 letters
Hermiswil bei Kirchenthurnen (BE) 26 letters
Deisswil bei Münchenbuchsee (BE) 25 letters
Guntershausen bei Birwinken (TG) 25 letters

Longest names with hyphens:
Vuisternens-devant-Romont (FR) 23 letters
Châtel-sur-Montsalvens (FR) 20 letters
Essertines-sur-Yverdon (VD) 20 letters
Valeyres-sous-Montagny (VD) 20 letters

Shortest names:
Au (AG, SG, TG, ZH)
Gy (GE)
Lü (GR)

And finally

Did you know that…?

…the only Swiss recipient of the Victoria Cross, the highest British medal for bravery, was Corporal Ferdinand Schiess. He served with the 3rd Regiment Natal Native Contingent at the Battle of Rorke's Drift in January 1879, and died at sea in 1884. In the 1964 film 'Zulu' he was played by Dickie Owen.

…the first bancomat (ATM) in Switzerland was installed in April 1968 at the Zürcher Kantonalbank in Bahnhofstrasse 9 in Zürich.

…the first Zurich telephone book, published in 1880, had 141 names in it. Telephone numbers were not introduced until 1890.

…the Helvetica font was designed by Max Meidinger from Zurich. It was originally called the Haas-Grotesk when launched in 1957 but the name was changed to Helvetica in 1960.

…the first part of the Swiss rail network to be electrified was between Vevey and Territet on 4 June 1888. The electrification was extended to Chillon in September of the same year.

…the Swiss football player with most international caps is Heinz Hermann (118) and the national record goal-scorer is Alex Frei, with 42 in 84 matches.

…Europe's first air stewardess, Nelly Diener, joined Swissair in 1934. She died the same year in a plane crash in Germany.

…the first self-service supermarket in Switzerland was opened by Migros on 15 March 1948 in Seidengasse, Zurich.

…Switzerland also has a league for American Football (as opposed to the normal football or 'soccer'). It was founded in 1982, has 15 Swiss teams and the current champions are the Calanda Broncos from Chur.

Abbreviations used

Cantons

AG	Aargau
AI	Appenzell Innerrhoden
AR	Appenzell Ausserrhoden
BE	Bern
BL	Basel-Land
BS	Basel-Stadt
FR	Fribourg
GE	Geneva
GL	Glarus
GR	Graubünden
JU	Jura
LU	Lucerne
NE	Neuchâtel
NW	Nidwalden
OW	Obwalden
SG	St Gallen
SH	Schaffhausen
SO	Solothurn
SZ	Schwyz
TG	Thurgau
TI	Ticino
UR	Uri
VD	Vaud
VS	Valais
ZG	Zug
ZH	Zurich

Others

AC	Associazione Calcio
AHV	Alters- und Hinterlassenenversicherung
AOC	Appellation d'Origine Contrôlée
BDP	Bürgerlich-Demokratische Partei, or Conservative Democratic Party
BSC	Berner Sport Club
CVP	Christlichdemokratische Volkspartei, or Christian Democratic Party
EEA	European Economic Area
EHC	Eishockey Club
FC	Fussball Club
FDP	Freisinnig-Demokratische Partei, or Free Democratic Party
GCK	Grasshopper Club (Zürich) Kussnacht (no longer used in full)
HC	Hockey Club
LP	Liberale Partei, or Liberal Party
NEAT	Neue Eisenbahn-Alpentransversale, or New Rail Link through the Alps
PdA	Partei der Arbeit, or Swiss Labour Party
SBB	Schweizerische Bundesbahnen
SC	Sportclub
SP	Sozialdemokratische Partei, or Social Democratic Party
SVP	Schweizerische Volkspartei, or Swiss People's Party
UBS	Union Bank of Switzerland (name no longer used in full)
ZSC	Zürcher Schlittschuh Club (name no longer used in full)

Acknowledgements

Every book is the result of more than one person's hard work. This one is down to my agent Edwin Hawkes and publisher Dianne Dicks, both of whom believed in it from the outset.

Thanks go to all my friends who contributed ideas and put up with my obsession with Swiss trivia, but especially to those who volunteered to help with the research: Christina Warren, John Sivell and Kathy van Reusel.

And to those individuals in organisations and companies who helped me despite my weird questions and nit-picking clarifications: Andreas Bauder, Hans Bickel, Dimitri Burkhard, Martin Cabalzar, Claudia Degiacomi-Küng, Adi Feller, Daniel Goldberg, Jacqueline Head, Alexander Keller, Melanie Kokott, Christian Langenegger, Samuel Leiser, Norbert Lüber, Natasha Luisier, Christoph Näpflin, Esther Nievergelt, Ralph Pöhner, Simon Portmann, Camille Roulet, Lisbeth Rüegg, Silvia da Silva, Manuela Sonderegger, Reto Tschirren, Michael Yates, Reto Zangerl, Roger Zehnder, and Paul Zehnder-Disler.

The Bundesamt für Statistik (Swiss Statistics Office) has to be applauded for its amazingly comprehensive online database and helpful staff at the end of an email. Hurrah for such Swiss efficiency. Thanks also to Präsenz Schweiz for involving me in the House of Switzerland, to swissinfo.ch for having such a great website, and to the Swiss National Library for its extensive collection of books on Switzerland. Here's another one for its shelves.

A special mention goes to Simon Denoth from RTR, Mario Schuler from Swiss International Airlines, Véronique Kanel from Switzerland Tourism, Wanda Bühler from Swiss Air-Rescue Rega, Daniela Fuchs from the Jungfraubahn and Martijn Mulder from www.onthetracksof007.com for all their help. Also to Jean-François de Buren and Hadi Barkat for a giving me a sneak preview of Swiss American edition of Helvetiq, to Bryan Stone for all things on rails and to Günter Bäbler for kindly letting me use his Titanic research.

And to my family for their support and to Gregor for making all this possible.

About the author

Diccon Bewes was born in the summer of 1967 in southern England (or more precisely at 50° 50′ 12″ N, 0° 46′ 46″ W).

He is 183cm tall, has size 42 feet and is only half English, which is maybe why he doesn't like tea.

His degree in International Relations from the London School of Economics (founded 1895) was awarded in 1989. His only other certificate is for First Place in the Three-Legged Race at his primary school Sports Day in 1978.

At the time of writing, Diccon has lived in Bern for 2,640 days so still has 1,740 more to go before he can apply to become Swiss.

He eats far more than the Swiss average 33g of chocolate a day but someone else is drinking his share of the wine as he never touches it.

You can find out more at www.dicconbewes.com

Bibliography

- *Autofahren heute/Driving today*, Verlag Heinrich Vogel, 2012
- *Chronik der Schweiz*, Harenberg Kalender, 1994
- *Heidi*, Johanna Spyri
- *Kultbuch Schweiz*, Rickert & Schlatter, Komet Verlag, 2008
- *Railways in the Bernese Oberland*, Photoglob, 2001
- *Reise auf der Titanic*, Günter Bäbler, Chronos Verlag, 1998
- *Schienennetz Schweiz*, Hans G. Wägli, AS-Verlag, 2010
- *Schweizer Geschichte für Dummies*, Georges Andrey, Wiley, 2009
- *Swiss History in a Nutshell*, Grégoire Nappey, Bergli Books, 2010
- *Swiss Watching*, Diccon Bewes, Nicholas Brealey Publishing, 2010
- *Switzerland in its Diversity*, Präsenz Schweiz, 2009-10
- *The Swiss and the British,* John Wraight, Michael Russell Publishing, 1987

Sources

Page

7   Bundesamt für Statistik, CIA World Factbook, Geofinder.ch, Swisstopo, Swissworld.org, Switzerland Tourism.

8   Passenger details from *Reise auf der Titanic*; Encyclopedia-titanica.org, Olympics official website, US Open.

10   Official websites of Australian Open, French Open, Roger Federer, US Open, Wimbledon; Daily Telegraph.

12   Bundesamt für Statistik.

13   Chocosuisse, Schweizer Bauer, Schweizerische Bauernverband, Swissmilk.

14   Historisches Lexikon der Schweiz, Swiss Federal Council.

17   Eurovision official website, Songcontest.ch, Nulpoints.net.

18   *Chronik der Schweiz*, Erstersteiger.de, Schweizerseiten.ch.

19   International Committee of the Red Cross.

20   Olympics official website, onlymelbourne.com, Swiss Olympic.

26   Postbus, Swiss Transport Museum, *Swiss Watching*.

27   United Nations official websites.

28   British Film Institute, Internet Movie Database, KiddieMatinee.com.

29   Bundesamt für Statistik, Bundesamt für Umwelt.

30   *Chronik der Schweiz*, Gemeinde Gisikon, Heritage History, Historisches Lexikon der Schweiz, *Schweizer Geschichte für Dummies*, *Swiss History in a Nutshell*, Swissworld.org.

31   Swiss Football League.

32   Berge.ch, Gipfelverzeichnis.ch, Swisstopo.

34   Eidgenössischer Hornusser Verband, Hornussen Epsach, IBS 19th International Symposium of Ballistics.

36   Carlos Leal official website, Daily Mail, Findagrave.com, Ian Fleming official website, Internet Movie Database; Location information courtesy of Martijn Mulder © onthetracksof007.com.

37   About.ch, Fifa, Historisches Lexikon der Schweiz, Internet Movie Database, Roger Federer official website, Saints.sqpn.com, Srf.ch.

38   Wakker Preis.

40   Die offizielle Schweizer Hitparade.

44   Ricola.

45   Bundesamt für Statistik, Internet Movie Database.

46   Swiss Federal Council.

47   Historisches Lexikon der Schweiz, Swiss Federal Council.

48   Bundesamt für Statistik, ETHZ, Swissinfo.ch.

49   Lauberhorn official website.

50   Swiss Ice Hockey.

51   Chocosuisse.

52   Bundesamt für Statistik.

53   Bundesamt für Statistik.

54   Bundesamt für Statistik, Swiss Transport Museum.

55   Swiss Person of the Year: SF1 (sendungen.sf.tv).

55   Street names: Telsearch.ch.

56   *Kultbuch Schweiz*, Naturhistorisches Museum Bern.

57   FAOSTAT.

58   Longest rivers: Swisstopo, Switzerland Tourism.

58   Islands: Switzerland Tourism.

59   Academy of Motion Picture Arts and Sciences, Internet
     Movie Database.

60   Political party websites: BDP, CSP, CVP, Die Grünen, EVP,
     FDP, GLP, Lega dei Ticinesi, MCG, SP, SVP; Bundesamt für
     Statistik, Das Schweizer Parlament, Federal Authorities of the
     Swiss Confederation.

62   Basel Tourism, Newly Swissed, *Swiss Watching*, Switzerland
     Tourism, Stadt Zurich.

65   Basler Zeitung, Berner Münster, Mobimo Tower, Prime
     Tower, Skyscraper City; Emails from Martinskirche,
     Predigerkirche, St Maria Magdalena, St Martin.

66   Map.search.ch, various maps & road atlases.

67   Bundesamt für Statistik, CIA World Factbook.

68   Federal Authorities of the Swiss Confederation, *Swiss
     Watching*.

70   Eidgenössische Kommission für Frauenfragen.

71   Solothurn Tourism.

72   Bundesamt für Statistik, *The Swiss and the British*.

73   Bundesamt für Statistik.

74   Bank for International Settlements, Britannica.com, Emersonkent.com, *Chronik der Schweiz*, Federal Department for Foreign Affairs, Globalsecurity.org, Kypros.org, United Nations official website, Universal Postal Union.

76   Company websites of Bally, Bernina, Caran d'Ache, Credit Suisse, Düring, Emmi, Freitag, Geska, Kuoni, Laufen, Logitech, Maggi, Mont Blanc, Mövenpick, Nescafé, Nestlé, Ovomaltine, Ricola, Rivella, SBB, Schindler, Sigg, Swiss Life, Thomy, UBS, Victorinox, Zweifel.

77   Schweizer Alpen-Club.

78   British Monarchy official website, Bundesamt für Statistik, Findagrave.com.

79   Die Post, Universal Postal Union.

80   Bundesamt für Statistik.

81   Amt für Betrieb Nationalstrassen, Bryan Stone, *Chronik der Schweiz*, Comune di Livigno, Eurotap, Historisches Lexikon der Schweiz, *Schienennetz Schweiz*.

82   Bundesamt für Statistik, Own research.

83   Bundesamt für Statistik.

84   Bundesamt für Statistik, Helvetiq Swiss-American edition, Swiss Center of North America.

85   Nobel Prize official website, Swissinfo.ch.

86   Bundesamt für Statistik, STATPOP 2010.

87   Bundesamt für Statistik, STATPOP 2010.

88   Das Schweizer Parlament, Eidgenössische Kommission für Frauenfragen.

90   Wanderland Schweiz.

91   Bundesamt für Statistik.

92   Bundesamt für Statistik, Gemeinde Lauterbrunnen, Starling Hotel, Switzerland Tourism.

93   SBB.

94   Potatoes - a national vegetable: Swisspatat.

94   American Food invasion: Burger King, McDonald's, Starbucks.

95   BLS, Compagnie Générale de Navigation sur le lac Léman, Hohentwiel Schifffahrtsgesellschaft, Schifffahrtsgesellschaft des Vierwaldstättersees, Società Navigazione del Lago di Lugano , Zürichsee Schifffahrtsgesellschaft.

96   International Committee of the Red Cross.

98   Schweizerische Bauernverband.

99   Bundesamt für Statistik.

100   Bundesamt für Statistik.

102   Victorinox.

104   Findagrave.com, Hofburg Vienna, *Swiss Watching*, Theroyaluniverse.com, Zentrum Paul Klee.

106   Bundesamt für Statistik, CIA World Factbook.

107   Swiss Mint, Swiss National Bank.

107   Gold reserves: World Gold Council.

108   *Chronik der Schweiz*, Weg der Schweiz.

109   Federal Department for Foreign Affairs.

110   Bundesamt für Statistik, Das Schweizer Parlament.

111   Council of States: Bundesamt für Statistik, Das Schweizer Parlament.

111   Flag: Federal Authorities of the Swiss Confederation, own research, Swissworld.org.

112   Bundesamt für Statistik, Das Schweizer Parlament.

113   U17 Worldbeaters: Swiss Football League, Swissinfo.ch.

113   Oldest Football Clubs: official websites of BSC Young Boys, FC Basel, FC Biel/Bienne, FC Etoile-Sporting, FC La Chaux-de-Fonds, FC St Gallen, FC Thun, FC Winterthur, FC Zurich, Grasshopper Club Zurich, Lausanne-Sports, Servette FC; Swiss Football League.

114   Tourist Attractions: Switzerland Tourism.

114   Down the Rhine: map.search.ch, Swissworld.org

115   Jungfraubahn.

116   City of New Bern, Helvetiq Swiss-American edition, New Glarus Chamber of Commerce, Swiss Center of North America, US Geological Survey.

118   Bundesamt für Statistik.

119   Own research.

120   Imports & Exports: Eidgenössische Zollverwaltung, FAOSTAT, Tradingeconomics.com.

120   Package pioneers: Thomas Cook Archives.

121   Foreign visitors: Bundesamt für Statistik.

121   Biggest Swiss Employers: Bundesamt für Statistik, Credit Suisse, Die Post, Economiesuisse, Eidgenössisches Personalamt, Novartis, SBB, Swisscom, UBS.

122   Own research, Swissinfo.ch, Switzerland Tourism.

123   Switzerland Cheese Marketing.

124   SECO Staatssekreteriat für Wirtschaft.

125   Autobahnen.ch, DRS Radio, License-plates.ch.

126   Swiss Football League.

128   Cantonal capitals: Reilefs.ch, Stadt Basel, Stadt Zurich.

128   Year of weddings: Bundesamt für Statistik.

129   Museum of the Swiss Abroad, Unesco official website.

130   *Autofahren heute/Driving today*.

131   *Autofahren heute/Driving today*.

132   Rega Swiss Air-Rescue.

134   Population change: Bundesamt für Statistik, *Chronik der Schweiz*, Historisches Lexikon der Schweiz, Tagesschau.sf.tv.

134   Trees: Bundesamt für Statistik, Federal Department for Home Affairs.

135   Foreign Lands: Comune di Campione d'Italia, Exclave.eu, Gemeinde Büsingen.

135   Watches: company websites of Blanc Pain, Breitling, IWC, Mondaine, Movado, Omega, Patek Philippe, Rolex, Swatch, TagHeuer, Zenith; Federation of the Swiss Watch Industry.

136   Lucerne Tourism, Verein für die Erhaltung des Museggmauer.

137   About.ch, Basler Verkehrs-Betriebe, Bertrand Piccard official website, Freediving.ch, Klein-matterhorn.ch, Koshertravelinfo.com, Rossiniere.ch, Smallestwhiskybaronearth.com, Swissinfo.ch, Swissworld.org, Tagesschau.sf.tv, The Times, Transports publics de la region lausannoise.

138   20 Minuten, Blick, Fifa, The Soccer Web.

139   Funimag.com, La Cie SMC, Seilbahninventar.ch.

140   Bundesamt für Statistik, Historisches Lexikon der Schweiz.

141   Brienzer Rothorn Bahn, BVZ Holding, Golden Pass, Gornergrat Bahn, Monte Generoso, myjungfrau.ch, Pilatus, *Railways in the Bernese Oberland*, Rigi Bahn, Rorschach-Heiden Bahn, Swissrails.ch, Schienenverkehr-schweiz.ch, Transports du Martigny et Région, Transports publics du Chablais.

142   Bundesamt für Statistik.

143   White death: Gemeinde Leukerbad, Gemeinde Tujetsch, Granat.ch, Historisches Lexikon der Schweiz, Tagesschau.sf.tv, ThinkQuest Library, Walser Museum.

143   Multilingual country: Bundesamt für Statistik.

144   Persoenlich.com, WEMF.

145   20 Minuten, Tamedia, WEMF, Werbe Woche; Email from La Quotidiana.

146   Veloland Schweiz.

148   Memoire-du-cyclisme.net, Tour de Suisse.

149   Most common surnames: Verwandt.ch.

149   Not Born Swiss: Filmreference.com, *Kultbuch Schweiz*, SBB, Screenonline.org.uk, Swatch Group, Zentrum Paul Klee.

150   AOC/IGP.

152   Blick, Eidgenössischer Schwingerverband, Kilian Wenger official website.

154   Bundesamt für Statistik, *Chronik der Schweiz*.

156   Switzerland Cheese Marketing.

157   International Dairy Federation, Switzerland Cheese Marketing.

158   Bundesamt für Statistik, FAOSTAT, Swiss Granum.

159   *Heidi*.

160   Bundesamt für Statistik.

161   Official websites from each canton: AI.ch, AR.ch, AG.ch, BE.ch, BL (baselland.ch), BS.ch, FR.ch, GE.ch, GL.ch, GR.ch, JU (jura.ch), LU.ch, NE.ch, NW.ch, OW.ch, SH.ch, SZ.ch. SO.ch, SG.ch, TG.ch, TI.ch, UR.ch, VD.ch, VS.ch, ZG (zug.ch), ZH.ch.

162   Aviation Safety Network, BBC News, Bryan Stone, Gemeinde Humlikon, GSoA, Historisches Lexikon der Schweiz, Schaffhausen Stadt Archiv, Super70s.com, Swissinfo.ch.

163   Chocosuisse.

163   Ten Swiss Chocolates: company websites of Alprose, Cailler, Camille Bloch, Frey, Lindt & Sprüngli, Maestrani, Suchard, Toblerone; Chocosuisse, Swissworld.org.

164   Historisches Lexikon der Schweiz, own research, *Swiss Watching*.

165   Comune di Livigno, *Switzerland in its Diversity*.

166   Bundesamt für Statistik, Lia Rumantscha, RTR Radiotelevisiun Svizra Rumantscha.

168   Historisches Lexikon der Schweiz, Swiss Federal Council.

170   Maps and atlas; RTR Radiotelevisiun Svizra Rumantscha.

171   Ten tallest dams: Grande Dixence Dam, Schweizerische Talsperrenkomitee, Swiss Federal Office of Energy.

172   Gemeinde Niederhelfenschwil, Ortsnamen.ch.

173   Bundesamt für Statistik, Historisches Lexikon der Schweiz, Linotype.com, Migros, Museum of the Swiss Abroad, Pressportal.ch, Rorkesdriftvc.com, *Schienennetz Schweiz*, Schweizerischer American Football Verband, Swisscom, Swiss Football League, Swiss Transport Museum.

Endleaf Swiss Psalm: Patronizing Association Widmer Zwyssig, schweizerpsalm.ch.

Facts & figures are the most current available from official sources, as of May 2012.

Index

About Bergli Books

Bergli Books publishes books in English that focus on living in Switzerland and intercultural matters. Readers who have enjoyed *Swisscellany* will also enjoy these Bergli titles:

Beyond Chocolate *understanding Swiss culture*	Margaret Oertig
Going Local – your guide to *Swiss schooling*	Margaret Oertig
A Taste of Switzerland	Sue Style
Cheese – slices of Swiss culture	Sue Style
Swiss Cookies – biscuits for *Christmas and all year round*	Andrew Rushton and Katalin Fekete
Lifting the Mask – your guide *to Basel Fasnacht*	Peter Habicht illustrations Fredy Prack.
At Home – a selection of stories	Franz Hohler
Swiss Me *humorous Swiss-American stories*	Roger Bonner illustrations by Edi Barth
Hoi *your Swiss German survival guide*	Sergio J. Lievano and Nicole Egger
Hoi Zäme *Schweizerdeutsch leicht gemacht*	Sergio J. Lievano and Nicole Egger
Hoi! Et après… – manuel de *survie en suisse allemand*	Sergio J. Lievano and Nicole Egger
Sali zämme – your Baseldütsch *survival guide*	Sergio J. Lievano and Nicole Egger
Ticking Along with Swiss Kids	Dianne Dicks and Katalin Fekete
Swiss History in a Nutshell	Grégoire Nappey cartoons by Mix & Remix

*Also available as an Ebook

Descriptions and ordering information can be found at
www.bergli.ch

The Swiss Psalm

(original in E flat major)

Lyrics in English: translator unknown

Melody: Alberik Zwyssig (1808 - 1854)

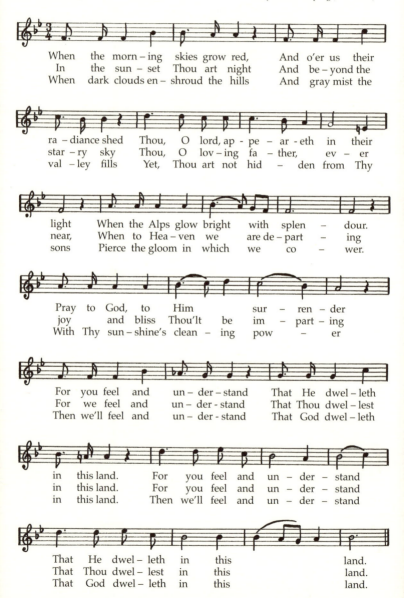